THE PSYCHOLOGY
OF BEHAVIOUR

A Practical Study of Human Personality
and Conduct with Special Reference
to Methods of Development

BY

ELIZABETH SEVERN
Author of "Psycho-Therapy"

NEW YORK
DODD, MEAD AND COMPANY
1917

CONTENTS

v

scious—Intellect our only Medium for Reaching the Interior Consciousness—Its Attribute of Discrimination renders it the Guiding Faculty—Comparable to the "man at the head" of any Large Organization—How to Train the Intellect—Development of Judgment and Sense of Values—Reasoning, Conscious and Subconscious—Importance of Logic—Intellect as the Supplying Agent—Intellect as the Adjusting Agent—Intellect as the Controlling Agent—Developing Attention—Importance of Sustaining it with Interest and Desire—Concentration, means of Development —How far Objective Matters should be made Automatic—Objective Control of Internal Organs of the Body—Value of Voluntary Passivity and Meditation —An Antidote to Modern Excessiveness and Over-Stimulation — Unconscious Rumination — Directed Thinking and Value of "Silence"—Intellect the Door to the Greater Possibilities of the Mind.

CHAPTER III

Imagination: *Reproductive*—Impressibility of the Mind—Memory, Conscious and Subconscious—Nothing is Ever Forgotten—A Good Memory Dependent on Concentration—Fixed Ideas—The Imaginative Temperament—Readjustment of Mental Images—Imagination: *Productive*—The Source of Originality —Imagination the Inception of all Action—Conscious Visualization—Two Kinds of Imaginative Thinking, a. The Aimless; b. The Directed—The Value of Reverie and Relaxed Thinking—The Imagination an Outlet for Repressed Energies—The Cause of Intoxication—All Mental Images must Materialize —Expectation Plus Intention—The Pathology of Repressed Imagination—Loss of the Sense of Reality —Education of the Child's Imagination—"Imaginary" Diseases—Dangers of Uncontrolled Imagination—All Mental Images Should Materialize in Action—Transmuting Undesirable Mental Images.

CHAPTER VI

CHAPTER VII

THE PSYCHOLOGY
OF BEHAVIOUR

THE PSYCHOLOGY OF BEHAVIOUR

CHAPTER I

SOME NEW ASPECTS OF MIND

THE PSYCHOLOGY OF THE UNCONSCIOUS

THE study of man's thoughts, feelings, and motives is a universally fascinating one. Even the least thoughtful of us love to watch and speculate upon our neighbours' actions and have sometimes an even greater interest for our own. Any extensive or careful analysis, however, of "human nature" has been left almost entirely to the great philosophers and moralizers, for the very good reason that the common knowledge of the human mind and its springs of action has been too limited and uncertain to allow of any satisfactory conclusions by the layman. Perhaps also it is because the race as a whole has been so engrossed with purely ma-

1

terial pursuits as to remain naïvely unconscious, for the most part, of the fact that it even
possessed a *Mind*.

Modern Psychology has now changed all this
and we are today embarking upon new voyages,
sailing for shores not too clearly perceived, but
with a serene confidence that the way is being
charted even as we go, and that we will surely
reach a goal.   There is no doubt but that the
present day interest in Mental Science and various psychological problems is one of the more
hopeful signs of the times and of man's general
growth and evolution.   The demand for authoritative literature on the subject is growing
rapidly and the greediness of the public for
even very poor food, if it but be labelled ''psychological,'' is a living proof of the need, and a
readiness for new light.

Psychology has long been taught after a
fashion in the Universities, but as the habit of
academicians is, in the nature of their case, to
stick tightly to what is called ''positive science,''
it has remained for a growing public to voice
its want of something more vital and ''appli-

cable" in this field; to bring out of the dry dust of polemical discussion into the liveness and activity of everyday affairs, the facts and principles which our researchers have long been labouring to develop and formulate.

Owing partly to its "newness" and partly to having been juggled at the hands of untrained adherents of the "movement," "applied psychology" is still suffering from many incrustations of ignorance, even in its own ranks, and still more from the prejudices of its misapprehending critics. That its greatest usefulness is yet to be developed is apparent, as so far it has been greatly hampered by the narrowness of the purely academical viewpoint on the one hand, and by the unwarranted claims of its enthusiastic but ill-informed adherents on the other.

The present work is an attempt on the part of the writer to elucidate some of these tangled threads, and to make a small but new contribution to a rapidly growing science—a contribution which has been developed through a wide experience as a practising Psycho-therapist, in a field where there is an almost unlimited opportunity for the study of human motives, needs and failures.

The viewpoint is frankly metaphysical rather than biological, and idealistic and suggestive rather than materialistic and "positive." Yet sight has not been lost of the need of exactitude, where it is so easy to be vague; and emphasis has been placed upon the *governing principles* of human conduct rather than upon its particular phases. Metaphysical questions such as the differences, if there are any, between Mind and Matter, the extent of their mutual reactions, or where one begins and the other ends, are not discussed; but that *personality* and its impulses are explainable, and that there is in the human mind a power which is definitely available for great ends, is the premise and main thesis of this work. This is not a new discovery; such has been the belief of the great thinkers of all time. It has merely remained for modern Psychology to furnish a better key for unlocking these latent forces of the human mind, opening up to our vision treasures and possibilities hitherto unattainable.

Foremost among these discoveries is the fact that *character* and *mentality* are *plastic* things, capable of indefinite modification—a simple enough statement, but of far reaching significance. There has long been a curious fatalism prevalent in our estimate of "character"; we have believed ourselves doomed to carry through life just that with which we were born —*character* being used in this sense to signify mental and moral strength and capacity. The idea of "developing" his faculties has never entered to any extent into man's estimate of himself, regarding as he has, his particular quota of instincts, traits, and tendencies, as either God-given or inherited from his long-gone ancestors and therefore, immutable. Strangely enough the faults and defects are all usually attributed to the poor ancestors, while even the Deity doesn't receive much credit for the virtues when they exist! The Idealism of today has fortunately made us more or less dissatisfied with "things as they are," especially with our mental equipment and our habitually poor use of what we have. The prevalence of the phrase "improve your mind" is a trivial but significant indication of the trend of the times.

Furthermore, we have not only come to believe in "improvement," but it is personal self-improvement that interests us most.   The tendency of modern education in all its phases is distinctly away from that kind of culture that comes by plastering on new ideas from the outside; it aims rather to draw out of each individual his latent and undeveloped faculties, much as Luther Burbank and others have developed strange and beautiful products in the plant world by studying the potentialities of plant life and providing different and more helpful conditions of growth.

The process of mental growth is not essentially different from that observable in all phases of nature. The force that works through the mind of man is similar to, if not the same, as that in the growing plant, the only vital difference being that man is a *self-knowing* creature and undertakes consciously and voluntarily that which in the lower forms is the product of a blind, instinctive life-force. The plant passes through birth, growth, experience, unfoldment and dissolution. It follows certain immutable laws and traverses unconsciously a whole gamut of experience. On another plane, human beings are going the same way, acted upon by great laws of which they have little or no cognizance, but hurrying nevertheless to the ·fulfilment of their destiny. This process takes place in every human life, but with this difference from the lower orders: with each degree of knowledge and awareness developed, more effort is required. Our whole progress and experience, whether we know it or not, is, and should be, an endeavour to obtain more knowledge of the laws governing our existence and expression, thereby enabling us to become Masters rather than mere pawns in the scheme of things. In so far as we understand this great principle and ally ourselves to it, bringing the pressure of our Wills and Knowledge to bear upon our problems, in so far will we achieve success in its highest sense and make real the ideal called the Superman.

To take up the question seriously of deliberately acquiring the mental and moral characteristics we desire, it is first necessary to understand the *implements* with which we have to work—*i.e.,* to analyse and learn to handle the various and complex elements of the human mind.   For this we must turn to the findings of Psychology, a field where in the last few decades startling revelations have been set forth concerning the hitherto little known workings of the human consciousness.   For, strange to say, such knowledge as we had in this domain of science was more in the nature of philosophical generalizations rather than a means for exact judgment of human thoughts and conduct. Somehow the *individual* had escaped being subjected to the microscope, whereas today he is the pivot of all our observations.   It is logical perhaps that an examination of man's mental activity should have been postponed until this late date in history, though it is difficult with our present array of material to explain why such important investigations with such significant bearings on vital personal matters should have been so long delayed.

It is astonishing to realize that it is only within the last few years that any serious, scientific, or widespread effort has been made to understand and classify the nature of human personalities with all their complex springs of action. There has always been an eager and universal interest in the few "self-revelations" that were available, all published personal "Confessions," and the like. But perhaps owing to its intricacy and intangibility we were slow in recognizing that the law of *Cause* and *Effect* must prevail in the workings of the human mind as elsewhere, slow to realize that given results were inevitably the outcome of certain causes. To establish any such law as this it was necessary to observe and tabulate the facts in a large number of individual instances, and from these deduce certain "averages" or conclusions. We now have well organized methods of psychological experiment, based on careful *Introspection* and *Observation*, which incomplete though they may yet be, have furnished us with invaluable material.

That man is able to study his own mind is indisputable, though naturally not all are equally successful in such an endeavour.   Certainly the more intelligent person can easily acquire a habit of dispassionate judgment of himself, and if mentally honest, can expose to his own view impulses and sources of action which were hitherto shrouded in mystery and alike inexplicable to himself and others.   To be sure, not every one is mentally honest, and likewise, those of an emotional or morbid bias would plainly be unfitted to report very accurately on their own ideas and feelings.

Much the largest portion of such psychological knowledge as we possess has come to us through the careful investigations of trained workers, and especially from researches in the field of "Abnormal Psychology," where in the study of mental pathology or diseased and disturbed conditions of the mind, we have gained through its very contrast our best perspective of what a normal and equable mentality should be. It is to the untiring research workers and medical men that we owe our greatest debt, for through them we have obtained our first clear glimpses of the workings of our own interior and intricate mental machinery. Psychology in its present form really had its first inception in the early French and English experiments in Hypnotism, which barely antedate our present generation. Back of this of course lies the monumental work of men like Spencer and Darwin, who by giving us a firm biological basis have enabled us to step more fearlessly into the realm of the purely psychic.

More recently we have the movement known as Psycho-analysis, defined by Dr. Putnam of Boston as "an attempt to make the facts and principles discovered through the analysis of individual lives, of service in the study of race history and of life in general." This is, of course, a broad statement and one equally applicable to many other forms of psychological inquiry. Furthermore the psycho-analytic *movement* must be distinguished from the psycho-analytic *method*, which is really a minor consideration, though the occasion of many hot disputations. Taking its origin in pathological studies made by Dr. Breuer, of Vienna, in 1881, and later by his brilliant successor Dr. Freud, Psycho-analysis today presents us with a large mass of scientific observations and theories concerning human emotions and experience; all of which has an important intrinsic value, and a still greater value as a light upon the scientific tendencies and momentum of our time. It is interesting to note in this connection that this most popular of the modern psychological movements had a practically simultaneous birth with the more thoroughly established and invaluable work of the great psychologists, Lange and William James.

The somewhat limited and arbitrary methods of Psycho-analysis and also some of its sweeping but unproved conclusions, justly have many critics and decriers; but however wide the mark some of its investigators may have fallen, and however erroneous some of their conclusions may prove to be, we must take the larger view and admit that as pioneers in a new and difficult field they have performed a great and needed service.

In my personal work with students I have at times used psycho-analytic methods with excellent results, though I do not say that the application of these methods has always, or even often, led me to the same conclusions as those of its originators. Like every independent worker in this field, I have developed methods of my own, which for my purposes and intentions yield far better results, especially when working with the individual for the alleviation of various mental and physical disorders. But we have the inspiration of their theories, which depart boldly from the old established canons; *only,* we must go much farther than Freudianism if we are to understand man's deepest yearnings and spiritual capacities.

We are led then to a brief consideration of the human Consciousness itself, since that is the field of all our operations. Fortunately we all have some idea of its nature, although clear definition is impossible owing to our being immersed in it, as it were, and unable therefore to gain the vantage point of a perspective. We only know it as a form of universal, undifferentiated activity existing within itself, having Being or Reality distinct from other phenomena which we designate as material or objective. Also we must believe that it is an expression or part of a greater Universal Intelligence of which we are only very small portions. We do not know therefore how to define it or where to place its boundaries because of its very infinitude and universality. Yet through the human process called Thought we are able to speak of it in symbols, to analyse and become somewhat acquainted with its manifestations, and to realize it as a sort of stream constantly pouring through us as an expression of that Supreme Consciousness which, we are all more or less aware, lies back of all manifested things.

Furthermore, Thought itself is not such an intangible and elusive thing as we have imagined. It should be regarded as a differentiated and organized form of *energy*, much like other forms with which we are better acquainted, such as heat, light, or electricity. It is necessary to understand something of this dynamic quality of Thought, in order to have any key to the psychology of man's behaviour. We often see the phrase nowadays "thoughts are things," which serves to impress more of their reality upon us, and is a very good statement of the truth, especially if we accept Herbert Spencer's definition of a *thing* as "a group of phenomena which *persists*." Certainly Thought not only tends to persist long after the moment of its creation, but has also the quality of movement or *vibration,* is in fact primarily an etheric *mode of motion.* It may be easier however to think of Thought as a *thing* than as *motion,* for it possesses definite and concrete attributes and effects, as does any other form of energy. It is also a power of infinite extent and is limited in its use only by our small store of knowledge as to its laws.

We each have a stock of Thoughts large or small, according to the degree of our capacity and experience, though of the major part of them we are mainly *unconscious,* owing to the generally undeveloped state of the intellect.

Those of which we are conscious concern mostly only objective matters, a knowledge of the internal life being comparatively rare. The affairs of the day are eating, working, sleeping, recreation—it is thoughts of these things with which we are most familiar and which constitute the bulk of our known mental life. In their very nature they are necessary and useful; but beyond them lies a vast area of mental activity—mostly submerged, it is true—and yet which is so great in extent and character as to contain within it the main balance of power— this is the area of the *Unconscious*.

The term *subconsciousness* has been bandied about a good deal of late years and used indiscriminately to cover all sorts of mental idiosyncrasies, likewise numerous books have been written to explain what it is, without much result in the way of elucidation. That we remain nearly as much in the dark as ever is not so surprising, however, when one considers the generic significance of the word *sub*-conscious, *i.e.,* below the threshold or out of the normal consciousness. Since it is not *visible,* and is

not easily reducible to the known mental laws,
many scientists have refused to examine it,
even denying its existence, and declaring that
all deductions concerning it must be by infer-
ence only, and hence not trustworthy.   This is
somewhat like having a gold mine which one has
never explored, and attempting to account for it
by declaring it isn't there.   To explain the hidden contents of the mind, one must first at least
admit their *existence,* and the theory of the
"subconscious" or the "unconscious," when
properly pursued, reveals them clearly to view.

The interesting thing about the submerged
phase of consciousness is that it can be mined
out as easily as gold ore can be extracted from
the earth, and indeed it is not unlike this substance in that it is a mixture of many elements,
both dross and precious metal. We must drop
the simile here, however, as the contents of this
mental mine are not solidified like those of a
material one—indeed, they are in a state of constant flux and commotion, with actions and reactions of the most complex and subtle kind
When once exposed to view, as they can be by

careful research, we have laid before us the roots and sources of all our thinking.

It is not that these unseen and potential elements are essentially *different* from the thoughts that are constantly in the foreground, but that they are more primal, productive, and intimately related to that unifying force, the Cosmic Consciousness. They are the stuff out of which our thinking life is made, though always *modified by our own past experiences in consciousness, both personal and racial.* Owing to its complexity and comparative invisibility, this deeper phase of human intelligence has been sometimes inaccurately marked off and set apart as an entity in itself; but such is not the case, there is but one consciousness. The lower levels of it should be regarded as a vast unorganized force which we are trying to harness and enlist in our service, an energy of which mankind has been hitherto but vaguely aware, but which holds within it all his potentialities for the future.

In the subconsciousness lies man's greatest gift, his faculty of apprehending *a priori* princi-

ples and of perceiving self-evident truths; in it
lie hidden all those cognitions having their
origin in the nature of the mind itself—cognitions, which though they may come to us
through experience, are really independent of
it. It is the realm of *Cause*—transcendental
Cause, one may say, since we know its powers
and capacities to be infinitely beyond our grasp
and comprehension. It does not seem so impalpable, though, when regarded in its true light
as the source of the faculty known as *common
sense,* that most *un*common possession, which
should be defined as the power of the *intuitive
perception of truth.*

In order to get some conception of the relation of the inner to the outer phases of consciousness, we might at this point best liken the
mind, with its many complex and varying elements, to a vast industrial plant with its
myriads of workers, each with his own little
circle of thought and activity but mostly unconscious of the vast product to which by his labour
he is daily contributing; yet his existence and
his work is none the less a necessary part of

the whole. Every thought and impulse that finds even a momentary place in the mind is equivalent to one of these individual workers, and an active part of the whole mechanism.

This illustration is especially good for the reason that we can so easily see how the purpose of an industrial organization would be entirely frustrated were it not for the control and management that emanates from the head office, in spite of the fact that the bulk of the work is done "below stairs," as it were. The superintendent of a plant sitting in his private office is not aware of all the detail and activity being carried on around him, and much of the accomplishment of his workers must necessarily remain unknown to him; for were he obliged to be aware of all these various acts his own usefulness would be seriously impaired. He has many assistants and sub-heads and managers of departments, all of whom have ideas and wills of their own and carry on their own part of the work without his immediate knowledge; yet while these helpers are for the express purpose of developing the general purpose of the whole,

we do know that among them often exists ignorance, inharmony, or even apparently wilful
disorder.   Such then is the state of the average
"subconsciousness"; it is this mutiny of un-
disciplined servants that calls for clear sight
and authoritative action on the part of the chief
and is so like to our own host of unruly thoughts
which would quite run away with us unless thoroughly disciplined and mastered by a controlling intellect.

Let us transfer this picture and imagine the
intellect, or reasoning self, to be the superintendent sitting in the office of the brain, and
further imagine the great concourse of mental
activity that goes on below the surface to be the
equivalent of the doings of the various departments with their several heads.   With this illustration in mind one can see the relation between
the two principal phases of consciousness, with
the necessity for a ruler at the head, that is, the
conscious Self or Master, to direct all employés
with their varied activities that are represented
by the subconsciousness.

The liability of servants to make mistakes is

proverbial, and it is no less true of these workers of the mind.   It is *not* one of the characteristics of the subconsciousness to be *infallible,*
though the disposition of some writers to confuse the subconsciousness with the *soul,* has led
to this incongruity.   Man is not only a composite of his past experience with its many
errors, but is a mere infant as yet, as far as his
mental and spiritual equipment is concerned,
and is therefore completely at the mercy of his
own erratic fancies and untrained forces, until
he has learned co-ordination and self-mastery.

Still further does my simile illustrate another
attribute of the mind, namely its *diversity,* and
its capacity for being split up into various seg-
regated elements.   Thus it shows itself to have
many aspects quite opposite in their nature,
each capable to some extent of independent
action.   It is thus, too, that one phase of the
mind may stand apart, as it were, and survey
the rest of itself, a faculty of the utmost service
when any conscious improvement or self-devel-
opment is undertaken.   Sometimes this capacity for *dissociation* leads to trouble and dis-

order. It is often the cause of mental and nervous maladies whose origin is to any but the trained psychologist obscure and baffling. It merely means *disorganization* and lack of *unity* in the general purposes, and calls for special analysis and reconstructive work.

We must not be dismayed that the very thing we are working to alter or improve, that is the mind itself, is also the thing with *which* we work —in fact, our only means of operation. That one may thus produce radical changes in the very medium in which he operates, with which he is obliged to work, is at first a little startling, but is one of the capacities of our organism with which it is important to familiarize ourselves.

The subconsciousness may also be said to represent the world of *feeling,* for in it we find the source of all our "predispositions" and emotions. Likewise it is sometimes called the "storehouse of memory," but might more accurately be said to be *the* memory, since nothing that is ever experienced by us, either outwardly or inwardly, is lost or forgotten. When we say something has "slipped our memory" we

merely mean it has left the upper level of consciousness and lost itself for the time being in
the darkness below.

In these subterranean passages of *Unconscious Thought* are to be found the remnants of
our primitive racial *Instincts,* which though
well-covered by the veneer of civilization, still
remain intact in most of us.   These supposedly
outgrown feelings frequently actuate us without
our conscious knowledge and furnish the unseen
motives for acts which are "queer" or unaccountable, though essentially *natural.*   Instinct
may be either "wrong" or "right" according
to the degree of our development and our relative place in life.   That is, an instinct which
may be perfectly right and useful for the savage, is outgrown and hence harmful in the
higher stages of development.   In any case it is
a heritage from our ancestors, and an important
subconscious element not to be lost sight of in
the midst of our complexities.   These instincts
relate not only to the bodily needs, but to all
the more primitive feelings, and are built up out
of the ages of experience which have preceded

us, an experience of which we would do well to avail ourselves for the most part, but which we lose or distort by a habit of smothering our natural impulses. There is the instinct for right food, for example—possessed by the animals, but largely lost in man; the instinct for outdoor life, for freedom, the power to detect danger—to mention but a few at random, all of which are very dormant, if not destroyed in most of us. When we recognize "instinct" and the primary reaction to life it represents, as an essential albeit unconscious *form of thought*, and cultivate it accordingly, we will have acquired a new and most valuable tool in the science of thinking.

All "feelings" have, in fact, their origin in the unconscious life and form much the most vital part of the mental organism. Elaborate and lengthy distinctions have been made between "thought" and "feeling" but a very simple one is to regard all feeling as an *unconscious form of thought*. As soon as one becomes really conscious of feeling, it rises into the realm of the Intellect and is there recognized and linked with the Will. Whether we should thus attempt to make all our feelings conscious ones or not is a debatable question, but in any case in studying the subconsciousness, it is necessary to recognize in it the foundation of all our emotional and psychic life.

That subtle power called *Intuition,* that is, a sudden ''knowing,'' is another faculty explainable only by a realm of unconscious perception. Whole trains of thought are worked out in detail and conclusions reached below the level of the conscious brain, which in minds temperamentally adapted for its transmission from the lower to the upper levels of consciousness, are flashed quickly at opportune moments up into the chambers of the Intellect. There it may be recognized and accepted, though not accounted for. Such results as these are more apt to occur in the quick and *penetrating* type of mind, but the important fact for us to note is that when they do occur it is the best evidence possible of that prescience which links the subconsciousness indubitably with the transcendent intelligence which animates all nature.

There are also many well-authenticated cases of *Premonition* where, by a still more obscure mental operation, events not yet materialized, or that haven't "happened" yet, as we say, are perceived in advance of their objective appearance. The pity is that we have allowed a sceptical, scoffing attitude or sometimes mere incredulity, to blind us to this wonderful capacity of the subconsciousness. We have counted the failures and mistakes that are often made in its use, for as a faculty it is both discouraged and undeveloped; and we have tried to explain by the unillumining word "coincidence," a phenomenon we would do ourselves far greater justice to investigate and study. There is overwhelming evidence to show that many minds have the potential faculty to perceive the shadows cast by coming events, or to describe current events taking place at a distance, of which they can have no conscious knowledge. It is due only to our stupid ignorance and fear that we have not long before now brought out of its potential state this delicate but powerful capacity of the mind. Certainly in studying the psy-

chology of *Behaviour,* we will have much behaviour to account for in the way of psychic
phenomena that cannot be accounted for without a better knowledge of the subconsciousness
and its extent. I was about to say *terrifying*
extent, since even our scientists seem afraid to
venture far into these uncharted paths. We
perhaps would not actually burn the witches at
Salem today, but we would in a more refined
way express our disapproval and our scorn—
and incidentally our colossal ignorance.

Inspiration as a psychological phenomenon,
being less rare perhaps than *Premonition,* com-
mands more respect, though hardly more understanding. We have all experienced moments of
comparative exaltation, when all our thoughts
seemed to flow smoothly as a river, and when
there was a sense of having tapped a reservoir
of force and feeling that seemed superb in quality and inexhaustible in extent. It is undeniably out of such states of mind as this that the
world's finest creations have come—the best literature, the great inventions, the finest art. All

action seems easy at such a time, for in whatever direction the interest may lie, there is a freedom from friction, a supply of energy, a fertility of thought, and a daring in action unequalled or even approached by any other state of consciousness. *Genius* is akin to this and is simply an uprush of the greatly extended powers of the subconsciousness. Genius might indeed be defined as Frederic Myers defined it in his "Human Personality"—as "a capacity for utilizing powers which lie too deep for the ordinary man's control." Undoubtedly the best work in the world is done when men obey their inspiration without themselves being aware that they are accomplishing their masterpieces —the greatness lying in their ability to open the doors and to function freely from the depths of their being—for *Inspiration* may be solicited, though not compelled. When unleashed, these powers are indeed so great as to make the man their servant rather than the master, and herein lies the danger and the penalty, since few of us are strong enough to even dare peer over the

edges into these magnificent abysses within, to
say nothing of allowing them to sweep us on and
up to great achievements.

In a sense this hesitancy and caution is a part
of the economy of nature, as we must grow
strong in order to wield strong instruments.
There is no reason, however, with the present
state of psychological science why we may not
all be uplifted by the flame from within and
have no fear. In any case it is not our part to
criticize or wonder at those great minds which
have finally been consumed or destroyed by
the forces which they once handled so valiantly.
It may be a weakness to go "insane" but at
least if one has tasted the fruits of high endeavour, a downfall may be considered a glory
rather than a shame.

We should remember also, that the subconsciousness of a child possesses practically the
same power and extent as that of an adult. Indeed it often seems greater, since the child is
more subjective, lives "nearer to nature," as
we say, is less artificial. For these reasons the
child's intuitive, imaginative faculties have a

freer scope, adding a charm and often a prescience that is the delight of all. Even in the
young infant there is the same potentiality, the
same bundle of intelligent responsive nerve-
cells, only not trained as yet in the expression
of their powers. If we would but talk to and
treat children with the same dignity and respect
we do the older people whom we assume to have
intelligence, instead of as though they were possessed of empty brain boxes, the world would be
saved much pain and useless misery, beginning
with the next generation!

An age-long puzzle is, of course, that manifestation of consciousness to be found in *Sleep*
and *Dreams*. Although science has more recently succeeded in lifting this strange phenomenon out of the realm of superstition, it is
still treated as a *physical* problem without
much consideration of its pure subjectivity.
For so long we have been taught that all dream-
ing was the result of some bodily stimulus, such
as a pillow pressing on the head, a creak in the
door, or a disturbance in digestion, that we have
been slow to come out of this materialistic con-

ception.   Elaborate theories have been devised
to explain these automatic reactions, and with
these unsatisfying dictums we were obliged to
be content, or else venture forth alone into
regions of the mind where all was thought to
be illusion.

Sleep being considered an exclusively restora-
tive function, it was thought that the automatic,
unconscious, and never-ending process of "repair" could not go on without the complete
cessation of both bodily *and* mental activity.
This theory is still being exploited and we are
all admonished to "sleep more" no matter what
our disturbance or our needs.   It is, of course,
perfectly patent to all that the sleep-state is a
necessary one and that when normal it is distinctly refreshing.   As a matter of fact man's
faith in it as a panacea for all his ills has a
foundation in truth, but does not explain, for all
that, what sleep *is* or what happens to the consciousness when it slips away below the threshold of our sight.

That Sleep is *not* the *cessation* from consciousness it is often thought to be, is perfectly

apparent from the simple fact of dreams, which are undeniably *some* form of consciousness, chaotic and fugitive though they may be.   Sleep is "nature's great restorer" simply because we pass therein into *another state of consciousness* which, by its passivity, completes the arc of our daily activities.   But we should not construe passivity as a void or a blotting out of con-sciousness.   It is merely another *plane of action,* affording scope for more relaxed phases of thought and sensibility than those normally expressing themselves in our waking state.

Either Sleep or Rest means a reduction in the amount of objective concentration and all volun-tary functions, and a corresponding activity of those phases of consciousness which are ordi-narily repressed during the day.   It is the alter-nate swing of the pendulum to establish the bal-ance in this world of dual manifestations and has nothing to do with repair as such, except as well-being on *all* planes always results in the maintenance of balance.   As a fixed bodily habit Sleep has become especially necessary owing to our highly specialized mental and physical activity, but its essential use will ever be to afford an opportunity, through dreams and reverie, for the normal functioning of the mind on a different level from that which is so obviously in use during our waking moments. It is, of course, another and important phase of the *sub*consciousness and an aspect to which our relation should be established deliberately and consciously.

Since we spend about one third of our life in this condition, what is more valuable than to find out what we can about our thoughts during the sleep period. Probably every human being dreams, a lack of recollection being no proof of the absence of such mental activity. The majority, especially heavy sleepers, do not recall dream-thoughts readily, but the occasional flashing out of some valuable bit of knowledge, as in a "warning" dream is significant as evidence of what may be occurring in this veiled portion of the life of the mind. It has remained for Dr. Freud and his disciples to properly emphasize the importance of dreams in the psychic life and to point the way toward the use of such knowledge for pathological and educational purposes. This is not the place for a detailed discussion of the meaning of dreams, or whether the elaborate symbolisms worked out by the Psycho-analysts are to be depended upon as throwing much light upon the real nature of the unconscious thought-life or not. Suffice it to call the attention of the reader to the *reality* of this unexplored region of his own mentality, as an aspect of mind to be observed, and to a great extent controlled.

The writer has completely reorganized the disturbed dream states of many sufferers, who were the helpless victims of unwelcome dream-images roaming unrestricted throughout their brains. Much of my own knowledge, and the solution of many problems, has come to me during Sleep—sometimes unsought, sometimes deliberately planned for; an operation not at all difficult when a certain vital awareness of the subconscious processes has been developed. And in Sleep, what a glorious freedom—one can close the door upon pressing actualities, and released from the limitations of the five senses, float away into that exquisite realm, where the unknown and the unseen is both known and seen.

Now that we have established the fact that the subconsciousness is not just a bunch of forgotten or casual thoughts tucked off in some dark corner of the mind, we will examine one or two of its principal characteristics from a practical point of view. The first of these was pointed out very clearly by Hudson some years ago in his "Law of Psychic Phenomena," as an *amenability to suggestion,* implying a certain pliability of structure which has important bearings. A knowledge of the fact that the mind, or some phase of it, is peculiarly open to impressions from without, is of exceeding importance, since it lies within our power to a considerable degree to determine what those impressions shall be. Through the impressibility and responsiveness of the subconsciousness to external impressions and ideas, we have a great responsibility, and at the same time a power of unlimited value.

The fact that definite concise statements could

be "suggested" so as to be received and *acted* upon by the mind of the subject with the greatest exactitude and rapidity, opened a new field in both Psychology and Therapeutics. It was indeed a great advance to discover that certain mental and nervous affections, or what were supposed to be diseases of the imagination, could be successfully treated by *talking the patient out of them;* though it seems odd that this plasticity and responsiveness of the mental organism was held to be a new and strange faculty. It appeared nothing short of revolutionary that a person's mental and moral nature could be altered by such a means. The wise "discoverers" overlooked the fact entirely that the influence of one mind upon another was of such common occurrence as to be practically universal; that in the relations and interrelations of life, no human being escaped the influence of his surroundings.

The truth is that *suggestions* are made to us all through life, from infancy onward, and even before birth in various tendencies impressed through prenatal influence, until we can truly

be said to be nothing *but* a composite of the
never ceasing play of the "suggestive" forces
about us.   Practically all our physical and mental habits find their origin in the behests of our
parents or in the customs of our community or
race; and as the subconsciousness develops long
before the discriminating faculties, we grow up
to find ourselves mere bundles of "suggestions."

Every word that is spoken by family or
friends has its bearing upon the tender mind
of a child—every habit of thought, every fear,
every inhibition is impressed, often indelibly, to
remain as a brand throughout life.   In the same
way a child living in an atmosphere of peace and
harmony, hearing only kind words and constructive thoughts expressed, absorbs this mental
food to his benefit and advantage.   All of us in
our younger years, and often in adult life as
well are the unconscious recipients of endless
"suggestions" of all sorts and kinds.   It is only
once in a while that we find a renegade, usually
the black sheep of the family, whose own vigorous personality is able to offset the many tend-

encies impinged upon him by his environment,
and whose inclination to make suggestions to
himself is strong enough to build up a whole
new set of circumstances, probably quite different from those for which he seemed destined.
Such a one may justly be said to have developed himself through "auto-suggestion,"
which sounds like a term of opprobrium, but is
really what modern Psychology has taught us
as to the way to reach and influence our own
subconscious processes.   As a matter of fact, it
has been the *method* we lacked, and the "discoverers" of the power of suggestion have been
mainly useful in the *applications* they have
taught us.

It is always a gamble to see whether in the
battle of life the innate qualities with which we
are endowed or the pressure of circumstances,
will win.   Certainly there is no better fortifica-
tion or assurance of success in either direction
than a knowledge of the fact that we are constantly absorbing ideas and feelings from all
about us and reacting to various stimuli, since
in such knowledge lies our only protection.   We

are then at liberty to choose our influences, and to close ourselves to such as would be otherwise overwhelming or detrimental. We merely need to realize the significance of these possibilities to be able to exert an invisible but potent faculty toward an unlimited strength and usefulness. It seems simple enough, for example, to assert *"I can,"* when the circumstances seem to make *"I can't"* not only nearer the truth, but inevitable. It is a powerful suggestion nevertheless, and if used earnestly is capable of working wonders.

Sometimes when working to change the structure of the mind by eliminating or reorganizing some objectionable mental habit, we are confronted with a hardness and inflexibility which is truly discouraging. Nevertheless it is fortunate that we *are* endowed with a sufficient amount of rigidity to offset the disintegration that would inevitably take place were we too freely acted upon by the various elements around us. The subconsciousness of a normal person does not bend too easily to whim or

caprice and it is a common fact that the older
we grow the more "set" we become.

It is thus believed impossible to properly
acquire a new language after the adolescent
period, and is no doubt also the reason why
Sir William Osler jocosely advocated the elimination from active life of all men over sixty
years of age. The trouble is that such statements are but half truths. The ideal mentality
is that which balances itself between a wise
yielding to impressions from without and a
stern rejection of all that is undesirable. Such
an attitude if cultivated may become so habitual
as to be as vital at sixty as it is at twenty; only
whatever the direction the "cultivation" may
take, perseverance and endless patience are required, especially if the mentality to be moulded
is of the "positive" type.

To understand *Suggestion*, or the action of
one mind upon another, it is well to consider it
as identical with an ordinary chemical process,
where one substance when introduced into, or
put into contact with another, produces a given

reaction.   Exactly the same thing happens in the human mind, though we are more often unconscious of the process than not.   A new force or stimulus from without sets in motion certain inhibited mental mechanisms, which were, temporarily at least, beyond the reach of the subject himself.   There is every reason then why we should learn this law in its psychological relations, as well as in physics, and avail ourselves of the knowledge by introducing the *right* forces into our world of ideas and guarding ourselves against the wrong ones.

As between teacher and student, or doctor and patient, it follows that there is a wider applicability of the law of *Suggestion* than in the individual working alone, for the reason that the teacher or doctor having a better perspective of the needs of the subject, and a more or less impersonal attitude toward them, is able to make his suggestions, or project his ideas, with a more positive force than when one is trying to be both the target and the archer at the same time.   We all know the exhilaration of being told by any appreciative friend that we can do a certain thing unusually well. It may be the whole means of enabling us to accomplish it, whereas we had believed ourselves incapable, and no amount of *auto-suggestion* in the form of "I can do it," "I know I can do it" would have produced the same quick and satisfying results.

Still, every action that we perform is the result of a previous thought, and if we take care first to develop the *right* thought before beginning, we can do much to make both thoughts and actions conform to our ideals without any help from others—provided, of course, we have learned to be "positive," for thoughts require force as well as good aim to be efficacious.

For the best results, however, the work of a Psycho-analyst is indispensable. He acts as an *agent* or substitute, upon which the patient can transfer his unconscious psychic forces. The doctor overcomes by his skilful *suggestions* the unconscious conflicts and disquietudes of his subject, thus serving as a *liberator* or *harmonizer*. Of course the whole force of a positive and carefully aimed *suggestion* may be lost if it is met by an equally strong opposing one. Unfortunately this is sometimes the case with a patient even where he thinks he is open minded and receptive and who listens obediently to various ideas, which though projected with sufficient energy to reach and benefit him, are completely annulled by some of his own subconscious or unknown convictions or prejudices. Thus a very "positive" or "decided" person may be difficult to influence by *suggestion*, even though he appears to be willing. It reminds one of the old question in Physics—"what happens when an irresistible force is met by an imponderable body"! The expert Psycho-analyst is, however, usually able to get around this difficulty.

There is also the person with the smooth slippery mind, from which *suggestions* glance off as from the surface of a glass ball—nothing is so annoying as to find one of these in one's own family! And then the type that drinks in eagerly every available *suggestion*, but has nothing but a sieve to put it in! Such a one is the most discouraging of all, for no amount of labour seems to suffice to stop up the perforations.   All these types serve to indicate the limitations of *Suggestion,* but they are limitations, it is plain to be seen, due to the nature of the patient and not to the principle involved.

There is no question of a "weakness of will" concerned here.   It is far better to be "amenable to *suggestion*" than not.   The rock-ribbed type of mind is slow to learn.   It remains too complacently ensconced behind the solid walls of its own beliefs, exerting itself only in efforts to *make suggestions to other people.* We all know, theoretically at least, how absurd it is to go about giving unasked advice, and we *should* know that it is equally futile to make "suggestions," no matter how good, when they are not wanted.

Perhaps this is the first rule to remember in making use of this psychological law—*i.e.,* not to make ourselves *moral mentors,* or assume the responsibility for *anybody.* The very first requirement for *suggestion* to *take effect,* is that the recipient should desire it enough to be *receptive.* If not so by nature, he can become so *voluntarily.* It may involve his *assuming* an attitude that is not *felt,* but very often by doing so he comes to a new and useful viewpoint not otherwise to be achieved.

In fact, we are altogether too much afraid of the power of persuasion and of being made to do things "against our will." If our wills are obviously working in the wrong direction, we should be very grateful for a person or a process by which they may be set right. If we are labouring under the weight of a wrong idea from which we cannot free ourselves, even though we may know it to be wrong, what a blessing that relief can be obtained through the intervention of another mind and another will!

It is not necessarily a sign of weakness to be "suggestible," it is rather an enviable state, for it implies an open and growing mind instead of one that is fixed, static, and hidebound.

There is a state of *over*-suggestibility which presents many difficulties, if not actual dangers. It is a type common enough to miss being called "pathological," but is nevertheless often very troublesome. For example, a patient of mine reports that she dare not buy anything in a shop

without first going home to "think it over," as
she is almost certain to be so influenced by the
salesperson as to purchase something she
does not want. This is plainly an extreme of
suggestibility; but how *can* such a mind be
helped into a stronger and more stable state,
except by the influence of *Suggestion?* The
form of treatment in a case like this should be
somewhat after this fashion: "You will never
be persuaded to buy anything you do not want
—you will always know your own mind—you
are perfectly sure of yourself—you cannot be
influenced by any one except when you desire."
Repetitions of constructive statements like these
will finally relieve the patient of her too great
susceptibilities and put her in a position ultimately to be independent of *all* suggestion.

This illustration will suggest the wide field of
this powerful means of alleviation for numerous pathological conditions which we have never
before been able to meet. Nor is it necessary that it should be limited only to profes-
sional use, for it is perfectly possible for a
person of even ordinary intelligence to con-

stantly apply this law for his own benefit and advantage. Furthermore, its use in the training of children is almost unlimited. I wish only to warn against the exceedingly shallow and short-sighted use that is made of *Suggestion* by many amateur teachers and practitioners, persons who have no eye for underlying causes and who by their methods, if they are not doing actual harm, are at least wasting their time in mere self-delusion.

To pour indiscriminate *suggestions* into a mind which is constantly creating new trouble and turmoil for itself, without the proper training and necessary reorganization, is like emptying little pails of water into the roaring sea, expecting some miraculous transformation therefrom. Here is where we find the real limitations of *Suggestion* and where other and more essentially spiritual forces are required to effect any material changes.

An aptitude for assuming the "other fellow's" viewpoint, at least tentatively, is not unlike the *will to believe,* as enunciated by William James. It is an attitude necessary not only when one desires to benefit by *Suggestion,* but is an important one for broadening one's life as a whole. It is deprecated by those who move through life with the one idea of avoiding mistakes, and who because of their very care and excessive caution miss most that is desirable. To many of these it may be temperamentally impossible to "will to believe," but to the fearless ones who take life as an adventure and are willing to "try" various paths, there is always the reward of a new vision and a new opportunity. Sometimes one climbs an unpromising hill, perhaps only half believing that it will lead him where he desires to go, but, willing to "take a chance," he finds on its summit that his hopes are more than realized by the enchanting vistas spread out before him.

Something like this attitude is essential to the mental seeker; the eternal critic, the sceptic and unbeliever, lacks one of the first and best implements for the study of the peculiarly delicate and evanescent fabric of the mind. There are limits to credulity, of course, which any sensible person will mark out for himself and observe; but above all, if one is to coax out of his concealed depths many of the treasures of the consciousness which lie below its threshold, he must have learned the secret of impelling his will in the direction of his expectancy and faith, he must have trained himself in the *will to believe.*

Such pliability should be possessed by every one and having once found and adopted this valuable and constructive attitude, it will not be difficult for the student of Psychology to follow me in what I have to say as to the *power of Affirmation.* "Affirmation" in this sense has a special meaning—it is an asserting or declaring to be true something which does not *seem* to be true at the time but which one desires to see realized. In the chapter on *Imagination* I will explain this process more fully, but here I wish to draw attention to the fact that to think scientifically, one must give up all preconceived ideas as to the *reality*—though not the *actuality*—of the fact-world; he must begin by assuming that what he desires to bring to pass *already exists in reality,* and that it is for him, by a definite and controlled thought-process, to project those ideas into objective and *actual* existence.

An *Affirmation* is making a definite statement of a condition one wishes to attain, as *though it were already attained.* This is using the Imagination and Intellect to shape and formulate the unorganized elements of Consciousness, and is the very foundation of all worth while effort to deal with Behaviour. To believe in and to aver a thing with confidence is the first step toward bringing it into being and completion, and can be secured only by constant assertion of power and capacity on the part of the doer. When once mastered it is an open sesame to the solution of all problems.

To the initiated *Affirmation* becomes an habitual mode of thought. It is a "positive" state of mind, expressing both *expectation* and *belief* and is not based on outward appearances. We all know the inspiring effects of asserting strength and courage where none is felt, of saying "I am able," or "I am not afraid" when both weakness and fear may be the dominant

sensations.   The nearer one can come to realizing these assertions of potential power to be the
realities, and the more one can train one's mind
to depend upon this mode of thought as a rod
and staff in the time of trouble, the greater will
be one's support and the higher the achievement.

It is after all only a mode for utilizing that
eternal energy which fills the Universe, a key
that unlocks some of the sealed chambers of the
mind and reveals how we may avail ourselves
of some of the infinite potentialities of the
Cosmic Consciousness.

CHAPTER II

INTELLECT

THE PSYCHOLOGY OF PERCEPTION

INTELLECT, in the history of Philosophy and Psychology, has had, as a term, various meanings and definitions. I shall use it to distinguish that comparatively small but important part of the mind which is conscious and *self-knowing,* the cognitive faculty, capable of forming comparisons and judgment. Because it is the practical, reasoning, obvious, everyday phase of consciousness and also the only one we ordinarily know I shall also call it *objective,* to distinguish it from those less tangible though more inherent phases of intelligence which we have just been considering.

Intellect is the mechanism by which we gain knowledge of the external world. Spinoza taught that knowledge might be acquired in four ways.

Hearsay
Experience
Reasoning
Intuition.

Intuition, as we have already seen in the preceding chapter, is the rapid and sure working of the *inner* consciousness. The other three in our list are the distinctly *intellectual* or objective processes, and the preponderance of their number is indicative of the extent to which we live in the *Intellect,* as compared to the more interior and instinctive portions of our being.

This is not to say at all that we are "intellectual" in the ordinary sense, but only that we have so far graduated out of the earlier stages of racial growth as to put nearly all the emphasis, at the present time, on external modes. Our "knowledge" is no longer a matter of inherent perception, as it once was, but a collection of *information* gained almost exclusively through objective channels. So far has this tendency progressed that we have come to worship Intellect to the exclusion or disadvantage of all the other powers of the mind.

Hearsay, to begin with, absolutely dominates the thought-life of the average person. Through the conscious brain are received, second-hand, the heterogeneous ideas of other people—accepted credulously, usually, almost as a religion, without even a question as to their truth or accuracy. Much of our education and even the reading of books, unless combined with an independent reasoning faculty, comes under this head.

Experience is a dear teacher and none of us entirely escape her hard lessons, but as few possess a mentality sufficiently active to adjudge her precepts properly, the knowledge gained by means of experience is often purely objective and an empty thing.

Reasoning as an active, conscious faculty is so dormant in most people, except in its most primitive phases or in its subjective aspects, that it does not play a very large part in their acquisition of knowledge; though by the great savants and leaders of the race it has long been held to be man's crowning glory and surest guide.

I hope to add my quota of emphasis to the importance of the reasoning faculty and especially to explain how it may be better developed; but while calling attention to this direction and possibility, I wish the reader to keep the true perspective by holding ever before him the foundation on which it is built, *i.e.*, the natural, logical, primal, reasoning intelligence, which though submerged and invisible is the inheritance of every man.   This inherent intelligence which is a symbol of man's unity with the All-Knowing Mind, is potential—the *Intellect* is but a handle for reaching it.

"Character consists in knowledge of the union which the mind has with the whole of nature" said Spinoza, yet we go on trying to "make" character by the most inadequate means possible—that is by rules and regulations which concern the outer life alone, by excessive contact with the mere world of *things*, scarcely ever with the inner world of *feeling* and *perception*, the world of Nature and of Truth.

Undoubtedly the inevitable period of ignorance preceding maturity in all lives, that is when the inner consciousness is yet unknown to itself, requires some rules and guidance for its conduct and unfoldment; but it appears that we become obsessed by these prescriptions, for most of us live and die without much knowledge of anything deeper than the superficial world of things, and are built up mainly out of hearsay, some experience, and occasionaly a little reasoning.

So far has this fetish progressed in modern times and especially in the Western world, as to very nearly exclude those valuable and exquisite attributes arising from the speculative and philosophical mind of the Orient. We are so overrun with the mere *doing* of *things*, with pride in material accomplishments, with "efficiency," "education," "business," "success," "getting-on," *etc.*, that we have practically obliterated the faculties of the inner life and lost the power of drawing upon our deeper selves for knowledge.

All of this is closely concerned with our undue exaltation of the Intellect; and though it is obvious that we require the very best possible

use of all our external faculties, it is my contention that most of the claims, and all of the
methods, of modern thought, and especially its
system of "education," are erroneous—erroneous for the reason that the true foundation for
all development is not recognized—which is,
first, that knowledge is already *inherent* in the
mind of man, and, second, it requires a training
of the *senses* rather than the Intellect, to bring
it out.   Not until these facts are firmly established can we proceed with safety to a consideration of *how to train the Intellect*.   And then
we must draw the distinction sharply: that the
brain-faculty is foremost in this category solely
because it is the *only organ* of the interior
life known to our consciousness, and that it is
nothing but a tool; and I shall endeavour by
pointing out its particular office to aid the student of *Behaviour* to make new and useful ad-
justments for himself—to reach, in short, those
greater depths within, which are, after all, to
be approached and successfully appropriated
only by an obedient brain.

  This view of the human mind as an instrument only, reminds one of the theory advanced by certain materialists, that the brain is like any other secreting organ of the body, only that it secretes *thought,* instead of bile as does the liver, *etc.* There was a time when I regarded this view as an insult to human intelligence; but after all what is the difference? If we but regard an individual life as an indigitated portion of a great, all-pervading life, we have a very good analogy; the brain is at best but an organ of the Intellect which in its turn is also an organ of other more important elements of consciousness; and the whole human consciousness is but an organ for the manifestation of a Universal Consciousness which flows through us like a stream, for purposes only vaguely comprehended by our finite minds. Which digression is necessary in order that when we speak of the Intellect as a monitor or executive officer of the whole mechanism, we shall not confuse it, as is so often done, with that essential "I" lying back of all psychology.

Perhaps the best illustration possible of the Intellect in its relation to other phases of consciousness, is to consider it as the "man at the head," the executor who sits in his office to control the volume of business that is represented by his organization; but we must remember that he is merely an administrator, and not the business itself; for though the power that is expressed through him is essentially the same as that in all his workers, there is the marked difference of *function* and *position*. He may, and should be, the sole director; if not, all his subconscious thoughts, feelings and impulses rise up to threaten and unseat him—not an infrequent occurrence as we all have occasion to know.

The Intellect might be likened too, to the engineer using his locomotive, as we use both body and brain as a vehicle for experience and progress through life. As the directing element of a powerful mechanism, an engineer is the equivalent of the Intellect. Through him the currents of power from the generative sources of his machine make connection with the body of the engine, just as the internal life, with its reservoirs of energy, is applied through the

Intellect to the external and concrete experiences of life. The engineer uses his position as executor to regulate both the extent and the direction of this power, thus paralleling the office of the Intellect with its faculty for judgment and discrimination.

It is exactly this development of judgment, or *a right sense of values,* that should be the main object of all intellectual training. And the power to consciously and efficiently operate the mind is as dependent upon training and organization, as it is in the case of the engineer. This is just what modern education fails to do; and the lack is the more pronounced in the mental world of today, because it is so strongly emphasized in the material world. Our *thoughts* are scattered and unrestrained: whereas they should be at least as orderly and easily ascertainable as our bank accounts or our libraries or the contents of our wardrobes: but to do this it is necessary to evolve a well-regulated personal *thought-system* corresponding in its careful organization to that in vogue in the best industries, in our homes, our clubs, and our charities. The contents of our minds are much in need of renovation, with the installation of a system comparable to the classified card-index of a good library. Not to know what one knows, is, to put it mildly, a drawback: and until we develop discrimination, self-analysis and impersonal self-judgment, we are in no position to realize upon our inherent powers and capabilities. Thus the first step in intellectual training becomes apparent.

Let us now examine more closely that distinctive attribute of the Intellect, which I have called *Discrimination*. It represents a selective power of prime importance, which a little thought will show, is not characteristic of the whole mind. The deeper phases of the thinking process are, because of their very unconsciousness, at the mercy of whatever winds may blow. Through the Intellect we have a handle with which we are able to guide and direct these forces, because with it we can discern, compare, choose, eliminate, and determine. It leads us for this reason, beyond and out of the

instinctive discrimination of the animal plane
and thus renders an important and necessary
service in our progress toward culture.

As a balance and medium for all the active
and positive elements of our being, Intellect is
paramount. Unless it is awake and alert, most
of the power generated in the motive centres
of the mind is dissipated through a lack of
proper control. For Discrimination means a
suitable use of our own material quite as much
as the selection or rejection of anything in
the outside world. And the especial quality of
the Intellect is such as to enable us to develop
the necessary *sense of values,* by means of which
all our other faculties may be utilized to the
full. It is indeed the *only* faculty by which we
may stretch to the full measure of our powers;
hence the exalted position rightly accorded to
it by all men of learning.

This does not mean, though, that a right sense
of values is possessed by all "intellectual" people, for they, even more than others, are apt to
mistake objective for true knowledge and elevate themselves with a false importance. All

of which implies, even in people of the higher
types, a neglect of this very faculty of discrimination on which they pride themselves, and a
stupid disregard for the really fundamental
sources of knowledge.

It is as though man had found such an enchanting toy in his unfolding mentality as to
become engrossed in admiration of it, forgetting meanwhile that *Intelligence* is a universal
principle of Nature, expressing itself through
any really responsive human machine without
regard to education or acquired proficiencies.
Yet my thesis is that our advantage is greater
with "acquired proficiencies" than without
them; and that with a *right* training we are less
likely to mistake the *means used* for the *end
sought* or the thing-in-itself. *Wisdom* we all
desire—Intellect may be the gateway to it, but
no more. How universally nevertheless do we
confuse the two.

To return then to a discussion of what Discrimination means, Emerson quotes the In-
dian Vedas in one of his Essays—"He that can
discriminate is the father of his father," thus

showing his opinion of the value enfolded in this power of perceiving differences, of weighing, comparing, balancing. Nothing in fact indicates a loss of mental balance so clearly as the feebleness, or absence, of the power to discern values—witness, for example, the mind of a fanatic or person of a single idea, where there is no discrimination—the result is narrowness instead of breadth, and inconsistency instead of poise, the ultimate end of which is insanity. All of us are a little "off" at times, when we lose the perspective and steadiness that comes from having a sure hand on the throttle of our engine. And we do not seem to realize that though the engine may continue to run for some time without the directing intelligence of the engineer, the inevitable end of such a course can be nothing but disaster.

There are all shades and grades of the discriminative faculty to be observed in human beings, from those who split so many hairs and hold such a tight rein on themselves as to scarcely move at all, to the emotional and unreliable type who go from one extreme of

feeling to another and accept all things good or
bad without even an attempt at judgment or calculation.   Too much discrimination leads to excessive caution, inhibition, and fear, too little
makes but a weakling and a weather vane, both
of small account in this world of competition.

We know very well how little value is to be
placed upon the opinions of those who lack this
important quality. They lose all the fine
points; "rave" over everything that appeals to
them: find it always "wonderful," "superb,"
or "absolutely great"; or else they condemn
with ruthlessness all that they do not like, never
knowing in either case anything but the extreme
degree.

The mind to be at its best then, must be able
to clearly distinguish and compare. Its capacity to mark differences is the equivalent of
the "feelers" or antennae of the insect, testing,
trying, accepting or rejecting, according to its
needs. The mind is a crucible, into which various elements are being constantly poured. The
reflective capacity of the Intellect enables us
to select and arrange these elements to the best

advantage. We are always in the process of choosing our environment, albeit unconsciously, and making our own reactions to it. If then in every choice this marvellous discriminative faculty of ours were at work, think how different would be the result, how many mistakes avoided and pain saved, how much more every move might count.

If we but observed even the same degree of fastidiousness for our mental food and experiences that the average person displays for his physical sustenance, there would be an immediate and astounding revolution. While more than considerable care and thought has been bestowed upon questions of dietetics, hygiene, housing, selection of occupations, *etc.*, we continue to delude ourselves with the idea that we are developing Intellect while continuing to feed it, without concern, on a diet distinguished mostly for the absence of nourishment and quality.

I speak not only of books and the generally wasteful reading matter with which people fill their minds, but of the material we are more or less forced to receive into our consciousness by

contact with the life around us—the vapid con-
versations, the hideous and stupid sign boards
that for ever confront us with their undesired
information; not to speak of wasted hours of
mental activity dignified by the name of
"amusement"; and the idle relations with the
thoughtless, the vulgar, or the stupid ones, who
circle us on every side.   Nor is this all; we deliberately embroil ourselves, or fall headlong,
into situations for which we have no real taste,
and frequently create galling personal bonds
which a lifetime does not suffice to dissolve;
suffering experiences which our souls bear witness are but superfluous stings of the lash—all
for no better reason than that we have not ex-
ercised the simple but most precious attribute
of *discrimination.*

These are but sketchy examples, which the
reader can develop as far as he likes, concerning the office of the Intellect as monitor, exercising its discretion as to what shall be permitted
to enter the mind from outside and what shall
not.   I think the few illustrations cited are sufficient to indicate that it is a function which, at

best, is very little used. In this sense the Intellect is a feeding machine turning over raw material to be worked upon by the constantly revolving forces in the mind—a machine that in most instances is sadly out of commission.

The significance of this widespread habit of intellectual inertia is especially impressive when one considers that by most psychologists the Intellect is regarded as the *only* agent of supply; that is, that outside of certain inherited tendencies, no impressions ever reach the brain except through the avenues of the five senses. If this were the case, and my contention be admitted that these senses are in the average person more than half asleep, one would be driven to the conclusion that we were all hopelessly stupid.

But fortunately we are *not* confined to the testimony of the senses only, for the acquisition of knowledge. We have the limitless source of Intuition, as we have already seen; and in addition there is no question but that innumerable impressions reach the mind by means of quite other paths—paths less material but none the

less effective.   I am well aware that the majority of psychologists reject this view; but as the
majority are avowed materialists, and refuse to
examine or admit the extensive evidence concerning telepathy and the transmission of the
finer psychic vibrations from mind to mind,
they naturally remain in ignorance of the fact
that Thought is so subtle a force that it may
pervade the ether like electricity and pass directly through what is called space, just as
messages are transmitted by wireless telegra-
phy without the apparatus that was once considered so essential.   Thus we have an undoubted and powerful means of supplying ourselves with mental material quite apart from
our original equipment of inherent knowledge
and the usual sense acquisitions—one to be
cherished and developed as the best possible
means of enlarging our horizon and increasing
our store.

But to return to the questions of intellectual
methods, I have already spoken of avoiding the
ingestion of undesirable or harmful material,
I now wish to call attention to the importance of

Elimination as a mental habit. Vast piles of mental junk are absorbed daily and yearly by almost every one, as we have already seen. Even intelligent people, either through general carelessness, or perhaps sometimes imbued with a blind desire for knowledge, have a habit of absorbing with avidity everything within their range. These extend all the way from the newspaper *habitué* to the studious ones who consume the public library.

By some kind of topsy-turvy reasoning all this is thought to be an admirable trait. What a fallacy it is, is shown by the perniciousness of the result—loss of the critical faculties and power to think for one's self. Even though the contents of all the books, papers, lectures, *etc.*, were *good,* it would yet leave the mind of the reader with a mass of indigestible material, most of which he can never use, and which as a clog to the wheels of his machinery is scarcely exceeded by any other one element in his life.

It is safe to say then that some nine-tenths of our reading matter, not to say our "affairs," should be eliminated—we could even afford to dispense with many of the *facts* now in our possession if we could but replace the space they occupy with the *power to think.* Life today is very complex and full of dangerous non-essentials. Just ask yourself honestly how many things you are now doing that you would be better off without and see if you cannot trim down your mind to advantage.

Let us turn our attention now to another aspect of the workings of the discriminative faculty, that is, of the passing upon and turning out the finished article, the *product* of the mind. There must be a *control* of *expression;* and the intellectual or discriminative person rarely ever "spills," that is, empties his mind, without care and forethought as to the fitness or wisdom of expressing his feelings and opinions, or without a forecast as to the probable result of his actions. There is an undeniable power implied in this reserve and he often leaves us wondering what else lies in the back of his brain. It is calculation and *finesse,* the product of discrimination and control—attributes never found in the primitive emotional types, who have not the power to say one thing while feeling another, or to express their feelings only in part. Some expression of the face or unconscious movement of the body is sure to betray their inner state even if it is not spoken in words.

Since the burden of my thesis is for greater freedom and spontaneity in Behaviour, rather than for restraint, I am not arguing the case in favour of those who can so successfully hide their thoughts, particularly as the ultimate logical outcome of this capacity is the quality of *deceit* which we all despise even though paying tribute to the cleverness it implies. We must admit that a considerable degree of Intellect is involved in all dissembling and that there are innumerable situations in life requiring the exercise of the faculty. Without discrimination of this sort there would be no such thing for example, as the "successful business man," and the popularity of the stage hero who succeeds in "putting it over" his antagonist by means of his "wits" is proof enough of its wide appeal.

Nor must it be forgotten that dissimulation is

to a certain extent absolutely required by the conventionalities of organized society, where it is politely called politeness. Whatever its basis, whether sympathy and kindness or merely self-seeking, the art of politeness or graceful social intercourse has its place and marks a degree of self-control and discriminative power which is in itself most admirable. Politeness is of course an acquisition of civilization. It is not a natural possession of either children or primitive peoples. They are swayed by their natural feelings with a serene disregard for the disconcerting effects of thus naïvely exposing them—which is one of the reasons we love them so!

This quality of frankness and naïveté has its own charm, and is indeed an ideal for the race to which we may hope to return—*after* we have *mastered* the Intellect. At present let us consider some of the advantages to be secured by the person who can hold his mental content in check, exhibiting to the world only that which his own higher sense of discrimination has passed upon and approved. With a criterion of this sort, both his words and actions may pass from a crude or destructive state so as to become uniformly gracious and useful. Such a one does not carp or criticize or speak unkindly of any one, or talk of illness and suffering, of accident, quarrels, or depressing things. He may have thoughts and feelings of all these things within himself, but he declines to add to the world's pain by producing them. Such a control is something to command the active admiration of all and can with advantage be made an unvarying rule of life. With the restraining influence of the Intellect one can exercise *selection*, even in the things he shall be spontaneous about, and cultivate *optimism* as a duty and a habit.

There is, of course, a danger in this: in the *persistent* optimist, for instance, there is an aggravating tendency—an intention to be "cheerful" at *any* cost, which frequently obliges him to exclude all the facts in the case and thus lose his perspective. Such rather than admit any weakness or physical infirmity, prefer to go on from bad to worse until help is useless; or they may cheerily assert that "everything is all right," when one knows quite well it is all wrong. Such an attitude *may* be the simple expression of a "stout heart"; but more often it betrays a serious lack of discrimination and results in unmitigated weakness. Perhaps the hardest thing in life after all, is to face facts as they are, for almost every one cherishes some pet illusions. The only way out of this jungle of error is through the proper development of the discriminative sense and the assertion of the power of the Intellect.

In addition to being the *supplying agent* of the mind, the Intellect exercises the equally important function of *adjusting agent;* for after exercising due care as to what we shall admit into our minds we have still to think about what shall happen after it is there. If troubled with mental indigestion or defective assimilation, as most of us are, it is no safer to neglect the signs and symptoms than it is in the similar case of physical disturbance. In fact, it is even more important to regulate the mental processes, as those who are familiar with my *Psy-*

cho-Therapy [1] will know, for the reason that the physical body and all its disturbances are but a reflection of its prevalent mental states.

To really achieve the habit of right mental adjustment requires some working basis in one's life, some religion or philosophy which supplies one with dependable standards. Most of the many sufferers who have come to me for help, whether the trouble were physical or mental, seemed to be floundering in abysses of ignorance as to the meaning of life and their place in it. The work of the well-trained psychologist is to help them find and establish some such relationship, for without a certain knowledge of Self, all else is superficial. Friction cannot be ultimately eliminated until its exact source has been located; but if an effort is made to harmonize discordant or puzzling experiences with one's deeper consciousness a certain amount of adjustment can always be secured.

To take up one phase of it, let us grant first that our mental material is derived mainly from

[1] See *Psycho-Therapy*, page 91.

experience; after which one must realize that
it is *what we think about that experience* rather
than the experience itself that counts. It is
the *reaction* we have to deal with; the mere
incidents of life, once past, are of little moment. It is the residuum or precipitate left
from our varied contacts with life, whether in
the imagination or actuality, that constitutes the
essential quality of the mind. This residuum
is due to the estimate made and the attitude assumed at the time of each occurrence. Every
action, every thought even, leaves its mark in
the subconscious memory.

Nor do any two people carry away exactly
the same impressions from any experience, no
two ever draw out of a book or a play or a
friend the same elements. Each is different—
some of the discriminations made are determined by instinct, some by reasoning and some
by other influences. But it is the reflection following—or possibly the absence of it—that determines what shall be finally retained in the
consciousness. If we would but take time to do
so, we could make our reflections constructive

ones, whatever the nature of the experience giving rise to them may have been. We can develop the "philosophical" mind, whatever our
temperaments or tendencies, thus learning to
erase the scars and marks of injury as we go
along, turning evil, failure, pain, and ignorance
into knowledge, power, and harmony.

It can be seen that to accomplish such an end
as this we must know both how to *discard* and
adjust, that it is as important to "forget" as it
is to "retain"; for our minds not only constantly collect debris, but we allow this un-
suitable material to remain indefinitely, with
no check to its corroding and destructive action.

Take, for instance, how many poor souls are
labouring under the burden of *regret*—regret
for past acts of their own, for lost opportunities, for the failures of friends and loved ones,
for the seeming injustice of fate; and although
we consider regret only as a "feeling," it gives
birth to many useless and impeding thoughts.
When memories like this come crowding up
out of the subconsciousness, as they so often

do especially in moments of quiet or reverie, it should be a warning sign. It is time for the Intellect to take hold and weed out the rubbish, to discriminate against or to adjust the manifestly conflicting elements.

What has been the mental process preceding the recollection of such unhappy thoughts? First, that the occasion that produced them was not met constructively, that is, with a balance and sureness and with the resilience of spirit necessary to pass through pain without scar. The attitude toward the experience was too limited, bound up perhaps with ignorance, self-pity, or selfishness of some kind, so that there was left somewhere in the consciousness an indelible mark, a self-injury, a rankling thought or feeling that continued to wreak vengeance upon its surroundings; otherwise no ''regrets'' could appear. And in the course of time, though the occasion of all this trouble may have been quite forgotten, the corroding action goes on unbroken, feeding back to the conscious Intellect a repetition and multiplication of itself until one becomes quite buried and lost under the weight of it.

It follows then that the power of the Intellect to discriminate and adjust should be deliberately applied in all matters of the Emotions, as well as in mental processes alone. Whatever may be the material presented, the Intellect should be able to so harmonize and adjust it with its own needs and laws of being as to entirely assimilate it; for it is only the non-assimilated material that poisons or causes pain.

The first step is to forestall future trouble by refusing to admit and harbour any disturbed feelings about the experiences of the present, and secondly by refusing to longer nourish and sustain those relics of the past already in the mind which on examination prove to be destructive. By means of this conscious self-knowing part of our mind we are actually able to uproot and weed out those obnoxious growths which we have so long nurtured. It should be a daily custom—not to look backward of course, but to keep in order our mental

house and garden; to adjust ourselves comfort-
ably and happily to each daily experience, and
never to go to sleep with any disturbing emotions to mar our rest.   With such a habit, any
chronic friction becomes an impossibility and
one of the greatest prerogatives of the Intellect has been fulfilled.

It is just here that the reconstructive work
of Psycho-therapy and Psycho-analysis becomes of such value.   While every student of
Psychology can do much toward the rearrang-
ing of his own mind, he should not be surprised
or discouraged that he meets problems that he
cannot solve alone.   It requires special knowledge and years of experiment, as well as an
earnest devotion to the cause to achieve the ex-
pertness essential to this delicate work.   The
practitioner of Applied Psychology comes to
have the same skill in solving mental problems
as the experienced constructive engineer possesses in his field.   Psycho-therapy is far from
being a completed science, but the imperative
need for exact knowledge in these more subtle
paths of the mind is so apparent that more and

more are the seekers after health, efficiency, and a satisfactory conduct of life turning to these avenues for the solution of every problem both personal and social. Perhaps the New Education will establish "mental laboratories" where every maladjustment or inefficiency will be scientifically treated after the manner of all the other special disorders.

It has often been said that what especially distinguishes man from the brute creation is that phase of intelligence known as *Reason*. If the reader has followed me closely in my discussion of the nature and the use of *Discrimination,* he will have already perceived that it is in essence but an application of the power to reason, and that it is developed to a greater or less degree in men according to their varying mental status.

Let us look first at the steps in the ordinary reasoning process, a sequence that marks all our mental activities in a way, though not always perceptible. To indicate it somewhat after the manner of Locke in his *Human Understanding;* every action of the mind requires first, *perceiving* the facts; second, *ordering* them; third, *comparing* them; and fourth, drawing *conclusions* from them.   Analysed, this is what we do in all our conscious thinking. Thus it will be seen that while studying *Discrimination,* we have come very close to that primary and distinguishing attribute of man's intelligence called *Reason.*   Not Reason in the Aristotelian or Kantian sense of *a priori* or intuitive knowledge, but *Reason* as the means by which the human mind *organizes* and utilizes its intuitive knowledge.

The first point that I wish to make clear in connection with the power of Reason, is that it does not belong to the conscious plane of activity only.   We are fairly familiar with its objective application, but we must now perceive it as an attribute of the *whole* mind, and recognize that logical, sequential mental action belongs even more to the subconsciousness than it does to the Intellect—a fact seldom realized or brought to our attention.

Not only this, but in reality *every mind reasons,* however immature; every thought or ac-

tion is the result of a previous series of thoughts
or actions, all of which are perfectly logical in
their sequence. Even "intuition" is really but
the result of rapid or instantaneous reasoning,
and though the original premise on which the
result is based may have been erroneous, making the final conclusion still more so, yet the
process is inevitably exact and without flaw.

This fact deprives intuition and all subconscious functioning of much of its romantic mystery. It is necessary that we fling away our
veil of ignorance in this respect and recognize
for once and all that the workings of the human
mind in all its phases are based on absolute
logic. To once grasp this truth is to dissipate
our old fear that instinct and intuition are un-
deserving and unreliable attributes—even if
the world in general has tossed them carelessly
to women and animals as inferior qualities.

But the power thus so lightly dismissed is indeed very profound, based as it is on nothing
less than the indubitable orderliness inherent in
the human mind. The frequency with which
we arrive at false or "illogical" conclusions is

due wholly to a failure to supply the mind
with right material in the beginning. Thoughts
do not "happen"; no matter how wrong, absurd, or inconsistent they may be, there is always cause for their existence. If the conclusion is faulty, it is certain there was somewhere an error in the premise, and the reason is
not far to seek: instead of searching out truth
with all our ardour, we are brought up on shams
and compromises—deviations are thus inevitable, our deductions partake of the taint,
whether we will or no.

If it were not true that the mind is always
logical, the phenomena of *Suggestion,* so constantly demonstrated in psychological practice,
would be impossible. Suggestion is a mental
process by means of which certain ideas are
projected into another mind to take the place
of those already there. It is the "influence"
of one mind over another and is a useful method
for substituting constructive thoughts for those
deemed to be erroneous or undesirable. It is
useful because it supplies a new premise and
once any premise is accepted by the mind, it

becomes a vital force productive of its own kind. And, as the nature of the mind itself absolutely requires the working out to a logical conclusion of any idea which has really found lodgment therein, we see the reason of expecting vital results from the insertion of a new idea by means of *Suggestion.*

Sometimes these developments are slow, or delayed for long periods of time; and again they are deflected by still other ideas or counter-suggestions which prove stronger. But when they work at all they work logically. To develop a proper technique of thinking therefore means a careful utilization of this natural power of deduction, by supplying and *sticking to* those ideas which we wish to see developed and acted upon.

We might define *Reason* as the power of *assembling* facts and viewing them in perspective. Essentially it means grasp. Let us consider some of our present day habits of thought that tend to prevent or destroy this valuable capacity. There is of course, the mind that is congenitally weak and unable to *take hold* of anything, a type in which even the best training might fail to produce any very specific results. But the most of our trouble is due simply to *not thinking.* Indeed we take such superficial views of most things that the veriest "dabbler" in any line may become a make-believe—and what is worse—a successful, hero, if he but pour out a sufficient volley of bombastic words to tickle the ears of the thoughtless. We are *mentally lazy,* too ready to accept authority, whether it be in religion, or medicine, or by the mere assertion of a self-appointed prophet in any line. It is so much easier to take the ready-made opinions of others than it is to exert our own forces to the extent of creating opinions for ourselves. We go to lectures to get quotations on other people's thoughts and we pride ourselves on becoming connoisseurs in the art of collecting other people's ideas.

In the same way do we all fall more or less under the spell of the printed page. Most persons need but to *read* a statement to solemnly believe that it is true, no matter how inaccurate or even absurd it may be. Our critical and questioning faculties are so dormant as to leave us almost helpless before the influence of any and every assertion. This is "knowledge by hearsay" with a vengeance.

Already I have called attention to the great multiplicity of things with which we have to deal in our present complex civilization, and the resulting confusion and incapacity to deal satisfactorily with any of them. It is clear that we must simplify life more in order to live it well; and in spite of a strong tendency to exaggeration and over-elaboration, there is at present also a steadily growing undercurrent of feeling for "reality"—a current that is sweeping away many of the useless and wasteful things of life.

This tendency is something that we should aim to develop individually however; especially by efforts to make *Living* a vital subject, a subject of which knowledge should be imparted in early life as of a precious art. We should aim for the adoption of simple, orderly, daily habits of thought and action, such as finishing things which are begun, or availing ourselves of the logical alternative of discarding them al-

together if not worth finishing.   In early childhood the mind should be trained until it is second nature to forget that which is non-essential
and retain that which is of value.   It should
be taught to see things in groups, *clean-cut*,
according to type and classification, it should
be led into the habit of perceiving the relations
that exist between all facts and all ideas.   *This*
should constitute the principal element of education, not a mass of mere information, nor
even a facility in dealing with information.
The Intellect is given us as a means of mani-
festing and materializing *Life*.   To this end it
can be seen how important it is that *Logic*
should be brought out from the dry tomes of
the academicians, and made a living vital *mode
of thought* for every one.

There is a steadily growing protest against
the mere *machinery* of living as it is constituted
today, to which it may not be amiss to call attention while we are studying the place of the
Intellect in human action.   There are so many
purely objective things seeming to *have* to be
done just to get through the day that the great-

est difficulty is experienced in making time for anything more satisfying or worth while. Most of us deplore this situation and yet continue to live helplessly under the domination of circumstance. There is the ubiquitous telephone, the much travelling about, the meeting of appointments, the watching of servants and employés, and for women, the tyranny of dress and household. There is beyond doubt a maddening multiplicity of inescapable detail attached to modern life; but the very intensity of the pressure of it should awaken us to genuine effort to organize our individual lives so far as possible on a different and better basis.

To do this one must become somewhat of a law unto himself, an individualist, a unit, a centre that establishes its own rate of vibration and determines the direction of its own activity apart from the social mass. To stem the tide of habit, convention, and universal custom, requires conviction and the courage born of conviction. It is not the régime for weak and uncertain characters, but for the meaningful life it is an essential.

There is no other handle by which to deal with these complications of living than the handle of an active Intellect. The discerning, discriminating, reasoning faculty enables us to see life as a *group* phenomenon, as a problem to be tackled where and how we will, and solved by scientific method according to our best ideals.

Assuming that my reader is ready to do this and seeking the way, I suggest a careful consideration of the following phases of Psychology which I am setting forth as a means to attain this end.

Attention is really the secret of all efficient action. The very centre of all vital thinking is the power to hold steadily to a focal point, yet the ease with which we are whisked away into unintentional paths betrays how little sovereignty we are used to exercising. It is a well-known fact that the power of sustained thought is the unmistakable mark of the forceful and well developed mind; though the *lack* of it is such a common characteristic as to occasion little comment. Scattered, intermittent or unruly thinking is the general habit; and when excessive is the cause of many nervous disorders if not of a breaking mentality or bodily disease.

Attention has to do with the *direction* of thought, and consists in centering all one's mental energy on a given point at one time. Angell defines it as "a rudimentary form of conation or will." I should call it more than "rudimentary," as it requires a considerable degree of volition, especially when the act is a deliberate, conscious one; but *thinking with or to a purpose* is not beyond the powers of any intelligent determined person. Being a self-initiated activity it naturally falls without the province of many, since there are those who seem to be minus the instinct or capacity for propelling themselves in *any* direction.

To chain the darting, lightning-like and complex movements of an active mind into something like definite concerted action, and concentrated power, upon a fixed point, calls for an effort of the will which is perhaps not easily self-imposed; but since to gain the power of voluntary attention is indispensable for anything like an adequate mental life, it follows that the effort must be made. Fortunately it is not so difficult as it may seem.

The first requisite to insure one's Attention being riveted upon the purposes in hand, is that *Interest* and *Desire* shall be united with it. And this co-ordination is the whole secret of the possession of the power of Attention; *for there is no trouble in attending to things which command one's interest.* The ingenuity and intensity of interest exhibited by a small boy desirous of escaping the infliction of an attendance at school, is a case in point; yet when set at some exercise in which he has no interest, his attention lags to such a degree that he appears to be no less than a dunce.

We have then two courses of action open to us: either to do only the things we *desire* to do, or else learn to *create an interest* in those things which we feel we ought to do. Both avenues must be pondered, for both will yield results and much can be promised when they are cultivated and mastered. In either case we are opening the way to the acquisition of the power of Attention.

Attention like every other conscious faculty has its subconscious counterpart which does many things contrary to our acknowledged intention, and is therefore termed *involuntary*. We receive innumerable impressions through the senses of which we are unaware at the time, discovering long after perhaps that our Attention has been most active without our knowing it. Especially is this true in emotional matters and it would be well were we always to review our thoughts and feelings of the day to see which ones have *stuck*. Sometimes we carry away impressions quite the contrary of those we have voluntarily admitted into consciousness; always these are the result of subconscious Attention bestowed unawares. Of course the real test in the use of Attention is to be able to *withdraw* it at will from any point upon which it may have become fixed, and *transfer* it to a desired subject. In the following chapter on Imagination we will see how this can be done.

There is also the kind of Attention we give to mechanical duties of various sorts, which might be called automatic, so subconscious or "second nature" has it become. By the cumulative force of habit one acquires proficiency through mere routine such as is afforded by almost any daily occupation or business. Constant repetition in any line of action tends to centre the Attention upon that line, until conscious Will is no longer required. Inability to place and hold the mind upon any new and unfamiliar subject is no occasion for discouragement, as new paths in the brain have to be made; but the *continued* absence of the power of Attention can always be accounted for by the absence of any vital interest—there are no associated emotions strong enough to sustain it.

In some of the modern Mental Science cults, considerable emphasis has rightly been placed upon the subject of *Concentration,* with many suggestions as to how to acquire it. Though the methods given are apt to be superficial and inadequate, yet the idea as a whole is most valuable, as perhaps no faculty is in greater need of

cultivation these days than this very one of
Concentration. Numerous books have been
written and published on "just how to do it,"
most of which give only too painful internal
evidence of an absence of the very thing they
seek to inculcate. Yet the trend is in the right
direction and if followed will help to simplify
and strengthen all phases of the mental life.

Concentration is but a highly vitalized power
of Attention and when active serves as a burn-
ing glass through which all the energy of the
mind may be centred with its full force upon
any chosen point. The value of it is obvious,
the means of acquiring and exercising it are less
so. The habit of carrying many things in the
mind at one time and giving only desultory attention to any of them is both common and
pernicious; one of the best accomplishments of
a trained mind is that enabling it to bring *all*
its force to bear upon a single point at will,
which cannot well be done if one has "too many
irons in the fire," mentally speaking.

Even the simple, trivial, objective things of
life should have our full attention when we are

engaged with them, though as a matter of course certain acts will become habitual or automatic and can be relegated to the care of the subconsciousness as completely as the act of breathing. Even these should not be dismissed until they have been concentrated on and thoroughly mastered. Thus it is well for the sake of discipline to try putting the whole mind upon such matters as dressing, eating, walking, *etc.* In the beginning it will be found very tiresome but this is only a proof that the mind is unaccustomed to being centred in an objective way.

When one has learned the lesson of doing things quickly and proficiently (which is not difficult with concentration) it is not only possible but an advantage to cease the close watchfulness and care—but not before. The Intellect is the leader—if everything passing through it were thoroughly *ordered,* all that dropped into the subconsciousness from it would be the same—even all our instincts and impulses would become orderly in time.

To develop *Directed Thinking* is the primary function of the Intellect. Careful practice in

simple *Observation* is a good way to begin.   Try
to tell what you have seen or heard each day—
to yourself; write it out, if need be to make it
clear.   Find out whether you have noticed
things and learn to take them in at a glance.
Glance at a dozen unfamiliar objects on a table
and see how many of them you are able to recall
—the difference in the results is largely a difference of concentration.   After training the
senses in this way, try the more objective exercise of *observing your thoughts,* and see how
many of them you can inscribe; tedious perhaps—but invaluable.

For some people it is very necessary to arrange their work on a schedule, that is, to provide a careful list of the affairs requiring attention and make a point of giving each thing
as it comes along its full share of thought to the
exclusion of all else.   This habit if adhered to
will do much to cure insidious mental weaknesses such as wandering, indecision or hesi-
tation; waste of time, inability to pass readily
from one occupation to another, and a general
disorderliness are all things that can be over-

come by the persistent practice of concentration.

There is a danger in this method as there is
in most good things, and those who by nature
are devoted to detail and meticulous habits
should take care not to allow themselves to fall
into the rut of hard and fast rules from which
they can be extricated only with difficulty.
There is a liability of placing so much dependence upon plans and regulations as to lose all
adaptability—the Will may even become inert
and unresponsive when not supplied with some
such assistance or stimulus. A pathetic evidence of such a tendency when carried to an
extreme, is to be found in the ex-convict, who
when released from a long siege of disciplinary
habits is more or less unable to formulate, much
less to execute, any adequate plan of life for
himself.

A number of methods are in vogue for developing Concentration which are in the nature
of mental gymnastics, and which when used with
discrimination have a certain value. Such for
example is the exercise of looking fixedly at any

small object with the idea of excluding all other thoughts from the mind, except those concerning it. The difficulty of doing even a simple thing like this makes apparent, not an inherent weakness, but rather that our methods of education are so faulty as to deprive the mind of its natural ability to fix the attention at will. This is especially true of women, who finding little in their customary daily occupations calling for sustained thought, are usually unable to devote themselves to a single line of thought with any success—especially if it be in the nature of an abstraction. One pity is that no stress is placed upon the Sciences in our popular educational curriculums—especially for women. Nothing is so efficacious as Science for the development of Observation, Concentration, Exactitude and Power—in short, for all that is implied in Directed Thinking.

The power to exclude unsolicited ideas and mental images, especially at such time as one is trying to focus the mind, seems in the beginning almost impossible of achievement, and it is only by recurring to the original intention with per-

is to begin developing an *internal physical consciousness*. Not of course, the morbid kind of attention which we frequently see bestowed by self-indulgent persons whose only interest is their symptoms; but there is a constructive attitude wherein it is possible to rescue from the abysses of subconscious oblivion a clear and certain knowledge of the action of all the organs of the body.

The practical value of such an accomplishment is perfectly patent when one stops to think of how utterly at the mercy of our internal workings most of us are. It is still more important as a means of organizing and integrating one's whole mentality. The physical body is the only medium we possess for touching life and the more thoroughly we master a sense of its operations, the more fully do we unite our subconscious intelligence to the objective consciousness. We have much to learn of the Yogis of the East in this matter, who by their wonderful knowledge and subjugation of the body proclaim their mastery of the Intellect.

Concentration when highly developed implies

a comparative anaesthesia to all other impressions than the one in hand.   Distractions do not distract, even the ragged edges of competitive thoughts gradually disappear until there is absolute clarity, and with it a feeling of great power.   It then becomes a state of abstraction, a subjective aspect of Intellect which should properly be called *Meditation*.

Meditation may be either an impalpable reverie, or it may be a dry, clear, coherent Ideation. In either case it is a form of Concentration, though comparatively very passive in its quality and in that particular quite the antithesis of the positive form of thinking usually associated with Concentration.   Meditation is not unlike sleep in its passivity, but it has the value of being a state entered voluntarily and for a given purpose and is one of the most profitable phases of the mental life.

It is as necessary to be able to "ruminate" at will as it is to add up a column of figures. What happens during rumination is a sort of simmering process by which assimilation and general mental unity takes place.   It aids perceptibly in the notice the mind naturally takes of its own operations—it is *Reflection,* the act by which the mind turns upon itself, to weigh and ponder its own thoughts and feelings, to realize upon its own unknown resources.

It is, of course, not enough that we should *think* and *feel* in a subjective way, for the logical end of this alone would be a self-annihilating sort of ecstasy—but to be able to look within with a clear, unshrinking gaze, and to make a habit of thus taking stock of one's mental assets and liabilities, is a mental function that should be performed daily—and *is* by the real quester. The voluntary meditative life is more essential to balance and usefulness than the much vaunted activity to which we are urged by almost everything in our environment. The need of *solitude* is not sufficiently emphasized— every one needs to be alone sometimes—and there should be a period of Reflection every night before going to sleep in which to revolve the matters of the day and put them in their proper places.

Furthermore, Meditation is one of the doors

into the Universal Consciousness—to go into it is like entering a beautiful room in one's house set aside as a sanctuary. It enables one to plumb the depths and richness of the thought world. It brings relaxation; without its soothing ministrations we are quick to tire under the high geared pace that life imposes upon us, and find ourselves with a paucity of that power and enthusiasm which alone makes life worth living. The word *Contemplation,* which best expresses the exalted mental activity made possible by Meditation, implies the going into a *temple,* the cutting off of the distractions of the world of sense and resting upon the poised centre to be found within. It also represents an entrance into that "silence" wherein may be heard the voice of Nature—it is thus very often associated with acts of devotion or communion, and is beyond a doubt the means of a perfect passage from the world of materiality and sensation into the world of reality and pure knowledge.

This interior world is unhappily closed to those who persist in living only in the world of things, but the subjective phases of the intellectual life come naturally to those of the thoughtful or reflective temperament. It produces the philosophers and mystics and is a great joy and solace to its possessors.

Even in the less intense and isolated forms, all intellectual action brings its own peculiar satisfactions. He who has it is never lonely or looking for occupation. Always there is something to "think about"; through printed pages the great minds of all ages are open to him, his friends and interests are not limited by time or distance. He often finds fascination in the mere study of words—symbols of man's thoughts and feelings as they are—and he is ever keen to increase his own power of expression through words, knowing that the channel of the Intellect is one of the most permanent and powerful of all.

There are, I suppose, people who "think too much." They suffer from a multiplicity of mental images, which are apt to be vivid and persistent, and which tend to a permanent state of intellectual *doubt* if not of actual bewilderment. They are tormented by a mental conflict which is as disturbing as an emotional conflict. They usually see both sides of a question at once and can argue equally well for the affirmative or negative; and though this capacity may at times produce both confusion and annoyance, it is a distinct advantage when it can be held in check; for it is true that the more highly intellectual a man becomes, the less *partisan* he is able to be. The "judicial temperament" is rarely if ever united to an insignificant intellect; but it needs strong sympathies and a unified Will to make it effective.

The ability to see a problem from all angles is the mark not only of "broad-mindedness," but is the essential point of departure for a student of truth. It is necessary of course to guard against uncertainty and vagueness but it is equally necessary to be as impartial and *universal* in one's thought as it is possible to be in this world of illusions.

Yet while I am counselling the development and more skilled use of the Intellect, I desire to show that the only true value in such de-

velopment is that of *perfecting an instrument.*
As an end in itself it is so little worth while.
Intellectual action alone, without emotion and
imagination, tends to fixity, inflexibility, and
artificiality. An example of this result is the
type known as the "money-maker," who
through calculation and shrewdness exercises
his intellectual powers to great advantage; but
this is living on the surface and has little in itself of satisfaction or permanent value. Not
but that "business" can be a noble pursuit, with
the best of opportunities for all one's powers—
it can even be filled with romance and poetic
feeling as well as practical advantage. But all
intellectual life, without the warmth and sensitiveness of the heart, without the vitality of
great purposes, without the touch of the "soul"
in it, is as dust and ashes.

For insight and power, for health and prosperity, for the realization of *all* our dreams,
we need *directed thinking;* but in the perfecting of this marvellous instrument of the mind,
the Intellect, let us not forget the greater
things that await ts usage.

CHAPTER III

IMAGINATION AND MEMORY

THE PSYCHOLOGY OF EXTENSION AND RETENTION

IMAGINATION, or the image-making faculty of the mind, is the power of presenting to consciousness objects other than those directly perceived through the senses. To understand what I shall say about it, the reader must dispossess himself of the common notion that it has any connection with the meaning usually ascribed to the word "imaginary"—that is, in the sense of being erroneous, impossible, or "unreal." True Imagination is not synonymous with *fancy* or *chimera,* but is, on the contrary, our most important constructive faculty and may be said to perform the initial and essential part in every human act.

Probably the reader is beginning to perceive, if he has not always known, that "man does

110

not live by his senses alone"; that he has an
inner life quite real and distinct from anything
concerned with outward experiences and impressions. This life is, from my point of view,
of such ultimate and supreme importance, that
I present these psychological studies principally
as a means of exploring its possibilities and
plumbing its hidden depths. To this end a
careful examination of the Imagination is vital, as it is pre-eminently a subjective function.

We are all familiar with the curious capacity
of the mind to re-present by means of mental
pictures the objects we have seen, or experiences through which we have passed. It is as
though at the moment of seeing or experiencing
a thing we were able to put on some inner closet
shelf an exact image or counterpart of that
object or experience; and by the process called
recollection we may enter that closet at will and
view its contents. Sometimes the objects
therein collected are more like jacks-in-the-box,
possessing concealed springs that cause them to
jump out at us in the least expected moments;
neither are all of these images beautiful or

pleasant to contemplate (hence the "family skeleton" to be found in some closet in every house).   But the fact remains that we do carry about with us a mental museum or junkshop which exists solely by virtue of the re-productive function of the Imagination.   It is this faculty which constitutes *Memory* and which we will consider first.

By reason of his capacity for retentiveness, man bears with him indelibly the marks of all his previous experiences—probably it is why he can never entirely escape that intangible something represented by his "past."   How can it be otherwise when he carries with him tucked safely away in innumerable brain cells, all that he has ever seen, heard, felt or known?

Indeed, if he did not thus retain all his past experience, he would have no standard of measurement, no faculty of comparison, nothing by which to judge present acts and thus "learn his lessons."   Furthermore, in his power of recollecting the past, lies also his power of constructing the future, and what is still more important, his appreciation of the reality of the present; for *time* and *space* are but creations of the Imagination, necessary mechanisms for projecting the interior concepts of the mind upon the screen of life.

The important thing to realize is, that however jumbled or vague our various impressions may be, they are never lost to us. The fact that they do abide with us and that under certain conditions we may have access to them, is our reason for claiming *Memory* in a sense not possessed by the animals. We should dismiss the idea that Memory is a *separate* function of the mind with a special "seat" in the brain. It merely represents the *impressibility* and retaining power of the mind and is the result of a kind of photographic process which is constantly taking place. If our powers of *perception, attention,* and *receptivity* are all in good working order, we have an automatic product termed *Memory*. Beyond this, Memory is hard to define, for it is like an aroma, as elusive as the fragrance of a flower—it is something "thrown off," from a normally functioning mental organism.

An inability to "remember" is but one of the many annoying evidences often forced upon us that our mental machinery is not running smoothly and that there is friction or waste somewhere. It may mean defective visualizing power, or it may mean mere disorderliness. Whatever the cause it can be remedied by the application of proper psychological exercises; for "loss of memory" is a simple psychological phenomenon of a pathological nature, a symptom of "sand in the machinery," which needs but proper diagnosis and care to be mastered.

Most memory-training "systems" overlook the real causes of forgetfulness and attempt to remedy the defects by purely objective means, such as the association between words, *etc*. Such methods are mostly props, if not delusions, and fail because they have no proper foundation, not being built upon any true knowledge of the mind. They may be useful in so far as they emphasize the necessity for a technique of thinking, but they do not supply the need to which they call attention.

A good Memory is really a matter of being

able to concentrate. Some people concentrate easily, it is a subconscious habit with them. Others scatter all their thoughts and thus blur every impression. For our mental pictures, whether the result of things seen and heard, or based upon abstract interior conceptions, must be vivid and clear-cut to be retained.

Whatever we really centre our mind upon, we are not likely to forget. The attention may be bestowed momentarily or even unconsciously, but it must be bestowed. When to this we add the power of *Interest* and *Desire,* we have the best and strongest mental images, the best conditions, for a good Memory. Even minor objective details can be retained in this way, if we but learn the secret of making vivid impressions at will, thus *stamping* the thought indelibly on the sensitive plate of the subconsciousness. Our thought force is usually so dispersed and therefore so enfeebled, that it is no wonder we are unable to retain much or accurately.

To keep any one thought or object in the mind clearly, it must be vitalized by *attention.*

In a normal well trained mind, this would not
need to be done consciously each time, though
as a step to that much-to-be-desired condition
of a "perfect memory" it is a practice not to be
omitted.

There is of course *involuntary* Memory, when
we retain pictures of things we have seen but
did not notice at the time, when images reap-
pear which were not created by any conscious
act of will.   Such occur more readily in connection with intense emotional experiences,
showing that in a highly sensitized state of
mind, the keenness of its impressions is greatly
enhanced.   Who has not thus remembered some
trivial detail, such as that in the midst of a
certain great emotional crisis he stood on a blue
carpet?

Certain hypnotic experiments have been
made, proving that the mind thus takes cognizance of and retains indefinitely many impressions without any conscious knowledge—
and these impressions are not always through
the eyes, or any of the senses for that matter,

though they add immeasurably to our store of knowledge.

Since so many of our mental images are involuntary and undiscriminating ones, unbidden reproductions of things that we have experienced, seen or known, the importance of undertaking a conscious and vigorous control of them is manifest. Memory is a precious possession, affording as it does a constant standard of comparison and a criterion by which to measure present activities. Also by means of it we can furnish our minds with all that is useful and lovely in life and enhance our pleasures to an unlimited degree, by being able to re-live them again in the Imagination, and by relating them afresh to all that we know and feel, until they present a whole fabric of iridescent beauty. But without a well developed selective power, without the control of the censor *Intellect,* we are constantly retaining and reviewing many useless, if not unpleasant or harmful, images. Most of us are quite swamped at times by unwanted and disagreeable thoughts and feelings which have had their origin in the past, and over which we seem powerless. If not mastered or dispersed, these may hold us like a cloud of black imps to darken all our days. Such are the "fixed ideas," the unsolicited impressions, that arise from an exaggerated memory, an over-susceptibility of the retentive faculty.

Fortunately unpleasant experiences like these can be avoided by the wise expedient of taking care to disperse the disturbing images at the time they originate. If such an effort were made every day, the time would never come when the mind was more like an old neglected cistern than the clear flowing stream it ought to be. We should take time to *arrange* our thoughts, with a view to *erasing the effects* of such as are not pleasing or helpful. There is a psychic process by which thoughts can be completely annihilated—and if not successful in this we can at least relegate them to the closet shelf in such a manner that they will no longer hurt or trouble us.

We often hear lamentations and complaints

of an inability to "remember"; but if the truth were told, there is far more suffering from an inability to "forget." It would be an unthinkable burden to have to carry in our objective consciousness every item of experience, every scrap of information, every impression we ever received. From this horror we are mercifully relieved in our capacity to "forget," or drop into the limbo of the subconsciousness that which we do not need in the present. Only, we don't even know how to forget properly, and many people carry with them all their lives the most undesired remembrances.

Nothing, as I have said, ever really leaves the mind, which has once entered it—and this should be a consolation to those who think they have "no memory." But to those to whom this idea is painful, I can offer hope, because the whole faculty of retention can be brought under the domination of the will in such a way as to distribute and harmonize all the impressions ever received. When this is effectually done, certain *forms* are dissipated and only the *elements* remain, thus freeing the mind from irritating images: there is no over-intensity on any one particular point, no strain or pressure to inflame the surrounding parts.

To make my meaning clear, I will give an example which we may all observe at times— that is, the after effects of severe grief or pain. Take two cases in which some personal loss may represent the same degree of sorrow and suffering. In one case there will be a complete, perhaps even rapid, readjustment to life. The sensitiveness to pain will be no less keen, the images no less vivid, but the final result will be as it should be, fairly complete internal harmony. In another case with the same circumstances, there will be an accentuation of the experience, a clinging thereto, an intense re-living of all the pain associated with it, until the balance of the mental organism is so disturbed that it stands little chance of ever being able to right itself. This is the type of mind that is apt to run to "fixed ideas" and makes endless trouble for itself.

With a combination of ultra-sensitiveness, over-intensity, and a lack of internal harmonizing power, much suffering and often irreparable injury is caused to the mental machinery. People of a vivid imaginative temperament should cultivate two things; first, a resiliency of spirit and compactness of organization that will give a healthy rebound from all shocks. This will provide the right reaction and thus enable them to withstand all misfortune. Secondly, they should take especial care as to what impressions they permit to enter their minds, and work assiduously to eliminate all the irritating and destructive ones. They should do all this and yet avoid *introspection;* using all their natural *tenacity,* or holding power, to keep the right pictures and to soften and sublimate the disturbing ones. Only so will these gifted people avoid much ultimate damage and confusion.

This readjusting process is all the work of the Imagination. We should understand that to merely blot a picture from out of the conscious mind is not real "forgetting,"—whether it be done voluntarily by great effort, or whether it occur accidentally and unintention-

ally.   To lose the power of recalling to consciousness at will something that was once
known or thought of, is annoying enough; but
to be unable to *reshape our images at will* is far
worse.   The former defect can be remedied by
better concentration and increased visualizing
power.   But to "forget" in the sense in which
I am now using it, means not only to drop
below the surface of the mind but to erase from
the total consciousness the *effect* of certain
original disturbing causes.   It is essentially a
process of reconstruction rather than obscura-
tion, and is a practical possibility because of
the creative quality of the Imagination.

We all suffer at times from a dislike of facing
disagreeable things and prefer to push them
from out the field of immediate consciousness
rather than to reflect upon them until their
power of annoying us is dissipated or mastered.
It is the line of least resistance and it avails us
little.   We escape nothing by it: on the contrary
we but increase the burden of that inevitable
day when the neglected unwelcome thought-
images come trooping back to mock us.   And

indeed they often do this work in secret, undermining the best of superstructures, as the Freudians have so well shown us. But for every enemy we have a weapon, and in this case a very powerful one, for the work of the Imagination is not only to re-produce, it is in itself a supreme productive agent.

There is nothing new under the sun, and *thought* is a universal substance, equally available to all of us. But there is such a thing as *originality*, and it consists in being able to *rearrange* all the images present in our minds, so as to produce a new combination. We have developed these images through experience, sense-impressions, and also by intuition or first-hand knowledge; and *no two people ever put them together alike.* Those whose patterns are the most unlike the whole mass or group-thought are the most *original*—and originality is the distinctive attribute of an active Imagination, an important phase of the productive mind.

Now it is quite true that we cannot conceive of anything which *is not,* that is, the *ideas* of which our images are composed are somewhere existent and always have been, in that immanent Mind or Intelligence which constitutes the stream of consciousness upon which we for ever draw. Our part is to give new shape and semblance to the thought-elements, which otherwise presumably remain undifferentiated and formless.

The inventions of the aëroplane and telephone, for instance, were conceived in the Imagination of some gifted mind. They are concretized forms of abstract ideas such as flying, floating, space, gravitation, sound, vibrations, *etc.* All these things come within the range of general experience: the perception and combination of them resulting in the aëroplane and telephone is the result of pure creativeness and originality—the invention of some particular mind; but the function is more or less active in all of us, and not confined to mechanical inventions alone by any means.

It is of course not difficult to recognize the creativeness of the Imagination in invention, or in works of art, such as music and painting;

but except by Psychologists the association between Imagination and the more ordinary acts of life is not so clearly recognized.

All psycho-physical activity is the result of previous psycho-physical processes, that is, we can perform no act that we have not previously been able to visualize. Not all these visual images are by any means conscious, as in the case of the child who instinctively reaches for food before he has been able to think out the process. Nevertheless, were it not for the possession by inheritance or otherwise of the mental image, no act would ensue. The efficiency of any act is very largely determined by the quality or vividness of the mental picture that preceded it, hence the people of quick, alert activity are the people of strong, clear Imagination. Whenever confronted by a problem their mind grasps the essentials of it and rearranges them into a product that is quickly translated into action—such never fail in "presence of mind."

In sleep we have a successive jumble of images which appear to be the most bizarre of inventions possible; the difference between these and the most finished work of art, which was produced by *inspiration* as we say, is solely one of orderliness or the reasoning process. Subconscious reasoning means the logical relation and sequence of mental images—it means *visualizing* in an orderly way. In other words, the creation of a picture which is held in the inner eye is the beginning of every activity— the inception of all accomplishment takes place in the Imagination.

It is important that the visualizing power be not impaired, as it often is, by various disturbances to the psychic life. One should be able, without difficulty, for instance, to graphically depict to oneself all incidents or feelings out of past experience that have any mental or emotional value. Things with strong emotional associations are naturally the most vital and clear, but mental recollections should also be vivid. Some people are not very successful in creating a mental image of persons or places with which they have been most familiar—even to close the eyes and reproduce in the Imagina-

tion an object just previously heheld is difficult
for some; but it should be possible to so dramatize all experiences as to make them live again
in the mind when one desires.   Train yourself
until you can visualize anything you choose,
from a rose to a complete Utopia.   Once accomplished, this power will serve you well; but
without being able to readily re-create what one
has previously experienced, how can one hope to
mould a clear well-cut model for any future
achievement.

To make a mental image not based on *facts*
proves a stumbling block to many, they can
only image that which is, or has been, present
to sense—all pictures of the future have for
them to be predicated on the actualities of the
present. If they are encased in limitations
and afflictions today, they cannot create an
image of freedom for tomorrow.   Such as these
find difficulty in availing themselves of the principles of mental healing, one of which absolutely
requires the formation of an image of health
in the mind of the patient, irrespective of the
present conditions.   It is surprising how few

people can think of themselves as being well if immediate circumstances are to the contrary.

If the would-be inventor of the telephone had said "the sound of the human voice cannot travel so far, there is no means of conducting it," he would have been stating a fact then existent; but his success with the invention was solely dependent upon the power of his Imagination to ignore this condition, and to conceive an original idea, out of "thin air" if you will, but in reality out of his own creative intelligence. Ergo, there is no greater mistake than to say of anything, *"it can't de done"*—unless one desires to seal its doom.

There are two kinds of imaging, the *aimless,* as in reverie, and the *directed,* as in reflection or any conscious thinking-out process.

Reverie has a definite value and place in the mental life and while if over-indulged it may become a source of weakness or danger, it is very necessary as the relaxing passive element with which to balance the more usual activity of the Imagination. The exigencies of daily affairs ordinarily require that we hold a tight rein and adhere to certain courses. As a contrast to this, it is essential that there should be periods when the mind may be permitted to roam of its own accord, when we may indulge in thoughts of things that are forbidden by the usual press of externalities—thus one may enjoy again the delights of some previous experience, or concoct new ones, made up half of hope and half of memory. Not infrequently one is the recipient of real "inspirations" at such times—the creative life being so sternly repressed by our constant and enforced activity, wells up at last to warm us with its greater richness and attractiveness.

Naturally, nearly all mental images are closely associated with the emotions, and the danger of too much "day-dreaming" or building "castles in the air" is obvious. Yet, were it not for the Imagination wherein repressed emotions find a natural vent, the pressure and friction would be very great indeed. Modern life gives but little room for the play of fancy, the poetic, the romantic, the mysterious, the sensuous—all are smothered or held in check.

The inhibitions of convention and the requirements of a highly organized society lop off so many avenues of natural emotional expression that the Imagination tends to become overcrowded with images of the affective or feeling life. Things that would never linger there become intense and even obsessing when physical and emotional activity is limited. Yet in the absence of normal, healthy avenues of discharge, the Imagination is the only outlet. It has indeed a true value in itself as a safety value and a respite from the restrictions that even normal life imposes; but the balance must be found and held.

Among the destructive habits that develop from a repressed Imagination, is the extensive use of drugs and intoxicants, common to all peoples. The means are dangerous and artificial, and the end sought is unrevealed to most of their users, but the result is, nevertheless, a liberation and expansion of the psychic faculties not so easily obtained, otherwise, in this world of materiality. The desire to experience, at least occasionally, the flights of

Imagination which occur automatically in certain subjective states, is practically universal. One does not, for that reason, counsel the use of artificial stimulants, only, it is well to understand something of the reason for their widespread prevalence.

The tobacco user speaks of how smoking "soothes his nerves," not realizing that he is thus expressing the need for some sort of suitable reaction from his artificial tensions. The delights of the opium user are well known. The same sense of freedom, which is experienced under this drug is also not infrequently induced by various anaesthetics which set free certain nerve centres otherwise inhibited.

The dangers of such usages, and the inevitable harm that results from forming a habit in connection with them, is not due to the alluring use of the imaginative faculties thus made possible, or even to the physical reactions, unpleasant and destructive though they may be. The real peril lies in the dependence placed upon an artificial stimulus, and the weakening of will resulting from so soon finding it indispensable.

That the call to free the imagination is strong, may be guessed from the frequency with which such means are adopted. The ease with which many people come to feel that such things are requisite should give us pause, and be reason for a careful study of the psychological process involved in the experience. Even a cursory look into this matter would be enough to prevent our grudging the poor man his glass of beer in which he is supposed to "drown his sorrows." Through the narrowness of his environment he has learned little enough of other ways in which to release himself from the constantly impinging presence of cold, hard facts; and little wonder is it that he seeks such solace as he may, in what is called the "cup of forgetfulness."

Medical men who work in the slums have reported that among people who are too poor to have even the glass of beer, or a pipe to smoke, they have occasionally found the curious habit of steadfastly staring at a lighted lamp, or other bright object, with the unconscious purpose of becoming self-hypnotized into comparative subjectivity. Thus unwittingly do the ignorant seek respite from the everlasting burden of objectivity and sense-impressions—an escape similar to, but not quite the same, as that obtained in sleep, where the Imagination is turned loose in dreams.

All these things show only too plainly the need for *directed* thinking in relation to the Imagination as well as to the Intellect. Obviously, it needs "free play"—but quite as clearly it is a force to be harnessed and subjugated to the Will. Especially is this true because the Imagination, more than any other faculty, leads the way in the formation of character and determines the *quality* of all our actions. It does this because it creates all our mental pictures, the prevailing ones of which materialize themselves in the personality.

There is no psychological law better established than the one concerned with the *materialization* of *Thought*. The nature of all thought is to *externalize* itself and this law requires that every intense image shall be actualized in some outward form. So strong is this sequence that it is not safe to admit any representation to consciousness if its subsequent external materialization is not desired. Fleeting and vague images do not of course have any weight and because of their lack of vitality die in the embryonic stage—but an *intense* and *unwavering* desire or mental picture is as certain to produce its counterpart in the external world as the day is to follow the night.

From this significant fact has arisen a certain cult that makes a point of telling you that you can "get what you want" just by "expecting" it. *Expectation* is a mighty force, but needless to say it has to be properly co-ordinated with many other elements in the mind before becoming usefully active. For one thing it must be united with *Intention*. A mere vapoury wish does not usually materialize itself, but an *intention* always does, if not deflected by other counter-elements.

As a matter of fact a clear strong image always implies an intention of some sort, be-

cause it is a representation of a *desire*. The
fundamental projective nature of desire will be
treated in the following chapter. Here we
have only to do with the imaginative powers;
but there is probably no fact in the whole of
Psychology that is more significant and profound than the one that shows us the Imagination as the source and starting-point of all our
actions. Every thought or concept that is conceived bears in it a potential energy that leads
inevitably to expression of some kind.

The concretizing of an image or idea always results in action. Usually this is direct,
such as the instinctive caresses resulting from
mental images of tenderness or affection; but
in the case of artists, or those of strongly
imaginative temperament, their haunting ideas
may take form in the production of a work of
art rather than in a direct physical way. Their
images tend to this form of creativeness rather
than ordinary objective activity, which accounts for what is called their "impractical-
ity." When such a tendency becomes extreme
the creator is over-balanced on the side of in-

trospection and subjectivity and there is a loss
of the sense of reality leading ultimately to
complete hallucination.

When there is an unequable or inhibited
state of mind in which the imaginative life does
not find its way out into some sort of expression, the naturally fluid state of the consciousness is interfered with and ends in a pathological condition of more or less seriousness.   A
detachment ensues from the life of fact and
objectivity, there is a split in the consciousness
which drives the sufferer still deeper into his
own involved imaginative processes and sepa-
rates him in proportion from externality.   If
taken in hand early, such a tendency can be
rectified and a marriage established between
the practical and the psychical elements of consciousness.

In children where the impulse is strong to
live in a world of their own creation, we some-
'times observe a loss of the sense of reality which
deprives them of the power of clear distinction
between subjective and objective phenomena.
They cannot tell whether the things they think

are "real" or imaginary—often the inventions of their own fancy appear much more actual to them than do obviously objective things. The greatest mistake possible in such cases is to imply untruthfulness or wilful misrepresentation; quiet reasoning frequently repeated, with suitable physical activity will serve to restore the child quite naturally to the needed balance. Indeed there is a period in childhood during the development of the imaginative life when it is absolutely necessary for him to be allowed freedom in the realm of his own Imagination. We should not forget that the very faculty we so often seek to curb is one of the most stimulating and precious in our possession and that ordinarily no pains should be spared to foster it during the period of its natural inception—that is, in childhood.

Instead of this, however, the custom is to disperse with the rude hand of "experience" or "mature judgment" the delicate and gossamer-like creations of the childish imagination. What buds we destroy that might later bear beautiful blossoms, there is no telling. Certain it is that by our impatience and inexcusable matter-of-factness, we often injure past all remedying the most vital spark in the youthful mind.

In the midst of the pedagogic babel of the day, one is able to discern but a few sane precepts for the cultivation of the child. Among these, however, is the important one that an objective education begun too early is a serious hindrance to the development of the child, as it strongly tends to repress his natural creativeness and destroy his equally natural subjectivity, wherein we know not how many beautiful things are being conceived and nurtured, which in the normal course of events would come to fruition later in life.

A child's education up to nine or ten years should ordinarily consist only of simple but true answers to his instinctive questions, with the addition of such toys or play materials as will afford scope for his Imagination. Among these are all the things with which he can build or construct, but the simpler they are the better, such as sand or wet clay, enabling him to mould and give form to all his simpler concepts. He thus symbolically expresses in its primitive form what he will later develop through the complexities of a more mature mental life.

The child's most valuable asset, that is curiosity, will not vent itself in destructive channels if he is supplied with the right material for his natural inventiveness. In the case of a very active or vital child, to supply this need requires some ingenuity in these days of civilized artificiality; but if parents would expend even a little time and interest in providing suitable material for their children, the next generation would be a surprising improvement on this one.

The child's whole growth is led by the development of his Imagination, and as he is usually more a product of his environment than anything else, his mental images as he grows older are not apt to exceed those of the people around him or of his station in life. He does not *expect* more than a certain quota and kind of experience and is therefore not able to produce it; which is a pity, for it is very much this quality of expectancy that determines the scope of a man's achievement.

If a child were constantly discouraged in his efforts to learn to walk, if he were told from the beginning that he never could or should walk, his Imagination would be so stunted by this treatment as to prevent his ever developing this most instinctive and natural function. And to face the facts quite frankly, nine-tenths of our illnesses and general inhibitions are built up out of just such training, by constantly hearing that we must "be careful" and "not to do this or that." By constant references, intentional or otherwise, to our mistakes, supposed ignorance, stupidities, and insufficiencies, we grow up with such a clamp on our Imagination as to be unable to *believe* in either beauty or proficiency for ourselves. What a degradation we have fostered here, only some one like a Psycho-therapist can know, who daily hears and sees evidences of various cramping and detrimental habits, of thwarted hopes, of deadened or perverted Imaginations.

Perhaps the reader will discern at this point some connection between what I have just said and the so-called "imaginary" diseases. *No* condition is *"imaginary"* if it *exists;* the fact that it may be existing only in the mind of the sufferer does not make it any the less real for that. Practically all the ills that flesh is heir to are connected with, if not the direct outcome of, a diseased imagination, so that those self-satisfied ones who pride themselves upon having a "real" illness, have much yet to learn as to what reality consists in. In any case the thought of disease has to be eradicated and the Imagination guided into more healthy and constructive channels.

The dangers of the excessive use of the Imagination have already been indicated. Since the exercise of it is a delightful one, it may easily draw our interest beyond its proper balance and lure us into paths not necessarily harmful in themselves, but which by their attraction may draw us too frequently and thus destroy the mental equilibrium and wholesomeness.

There are natures very prone to this habit, natures lacking usually in strong physical qualities, so that the inclination to *think* about things rather than *do* them is a very pleasing one. We thus see developed habits of vagueness and uncertainty, with a corresponding lack of the power of execution. It is so easy by means of the Imagination to dramatize one's thoughts and experiences, it calls for so little exertion and holds such peculiar satisfactions of its own, that there is a real and insidious harm in allowing this tendency to go unchecked.

Particularly is this true where the scenes and sensations depicted in the mind are more especially concerned with the inhibited impulses and emotional tendencies. The most deleterious habits are often formed this way which—and to this I wish to call special attention—are injurious, not because of the emotions concerned in them, not even because they so often relate to the sex life, but because being the uprisings of instincts and passions which can find no expression in the normal, physical life, they are all diverted into and overburden the channels of the Imagination.

That there must be an outlet of some kind is obvious, and that this escape valve is automatically furnished by means of the internal psychic life is equally obvious. This is in itself perfectly right and normal—the injury arises from the fact that all our mental images should exist for the sole purpose of initiating concrete acts in the world of materiality, and are intended to precede and dominate the objective life.

What we *cannot* for one reason or another express in the world of materiality, we must find some adjustment for. Simple repression is usually resorted to, but repression alone is dangerous. The original image must be destroyed, blotted out; and the desire which gave it birth must be transmuted into another form.

On the whole, it is essential to know and abide by this rule—that any idea, feeling, or sentiment recognized as arising from within, which does not take form in *action,* which does not

express itself in fact or deed, is certain to react upon the mental organism to its serious
detriment.   If strong it will ferment and poison
the system; if weak, it will evaporate into mere
nothingness before it can be used.   The modern slogan of "do it now" has its value—and
should be supplemented by *"or set it right."*
To intend to do a thing, to hold the mental picture of it and yet never really do it, is about
as subversive of real progress as anything well
can be.   Perhaps the only thing that is worse is
to hold on to the image and *worry* over it.   Far
better would it be never to have conceived the
idea than to prevent its birth, after the conception.   But then the world is full of abortiveness.

There is in us all, nevertheless, an undying
desire to transcend the monotones of life; a
strong wish to *do* and *be* something.   We long
to break the limits of our horizon, knowing instinctively that we have lived too closely bound
to earth, scarcely daring to expand to our full
height.   We crave *excitement,* which is but one
way of saying how tired we are of the prairie

tameness stretching out on every side. We live in the utmost matter-of-factness—imprisoned by our devotion to utilitarianism—when life might be one great and unending adventure.

The answer is, *cherish your Imagination.* Let it take you across the Alps of your hopes, never failing to follow it as closely as a shadow, The power of your mind to conceive, construct and produce is but an augury and a promise: *believe* in it, trust your aspirations; and in that time will all your dreams "come true."

CHAPTER IV

WILL

THE PSYCHOLOGY OF ACTION

Trust in thine own untried capacity,
As thou wouldst trust in God Himself.
Thy soul is but an emanation from the whole.
Thou dost not dream what forces lie in thee,
Vast and unfathomed as the grandest sea.
Thy silent mind o'er diamond caves may roll;
Go seek them; but let pilot Will control
Those passions which thy favouring winds can be.
No man shall place a limit to thy strength;
Such triumphs as no mortal ever gained
May yet be thine if thou wilt but believe
In thy Creator and thyself—
At length, some feet will tread all heights now unattained—
Why not thine own?
Press on; Achieve! Achieve!

                                        E. W. WILCOX.

WILL—is there a word more full of magic?
Does it not contain enfolded within its silent
depths almost all that we can conceive of as being desirable? For it implies *power,* and with
power what does it matter with what obstacles

146

we are confronted, what problems we are asked
to solve?

That there is good reason for this universal
feeling of respect for Will, I shall seek to show;
for in its last analysis this towering attribute
of man represents the original capacity of the
soul, and can be defined as nothing less than
the impulse of Life itself, of origin mysterious
and divine.

Let us clear our horizon at once of the limited
view of Will which conceives of it as mere
dominating selfishness, a power to master or
influence others, or an unreasoning stubborn-
ness. Let us also be rid of the concept which
visions a person of Will as a sort of frozen au-
tomaton, a being in whom cold intellect super-
sedes all natural human instinct and emotion.
Resistlessness is indeed an attribute of the
will-ful person, but true Will is far deeper than
all matters of intellect or emotion.

Will is *the machinery for converting the
static energies of the soul into dynamic power,*
a means of accelerating and expressing the
Life-urge in every human being. It leads in-

evitably into action, it consummates—it is in fact, the exact point of application of the abstract cosmic energy to human life. Or, it may be visualized as a galvanic thread on which all the activities of life are strung and the force by which they are energized. Indeed, so profound is Will in its nature that it has been expressed by some of the philosophers as being synonymous with God. It is this essentially spiritual nature of Will that I wish to emphasize, as I consider such a conception the only one leading to any proper understanding or use of it.

If we see Will as a spontaneous expression of a deep inner force, a force which animates every life and all Life, a *Supreme Urge* in fact, we can for one thing, *trust* it. If we as human beings are, as I conceive it, exfoliations of the Divine Mind or Supreme Being, we are also expressions of the *Supreme Will,* and have, in our *power to will,* a divine manifestation or "spark"; a faculty which should be as a guiding star, a criterion, a force upon which to depend, an unfailing power with which to hew our way through life. In it we find our *raison d'être,* and because of it we should dare to believe in the expression and fulfilment of our desires.

Even that much-prized and elusive thing, a "personality," is almost wholly dependent upon the degree of development of the Will—certainly a will-less person cannot be said to have a personality—and the absence of it indicates more than anything else, a characterless being, so lacking in magnetism and direction as to be usually passed by unnoticed.

This wonderful endowment then, this Will that impels us to work, to live, to love, in fact to all expression and accomplishment, is simply the *life-force in action;* the same as Bergson's *élan vital,* and Freud's *Libido.* To make it more concrete, I shall define it as *Desire in Action.*

Let us look into the generic meaning of *Desire.* In its largest sense, it will be seen to be the *volition of the universal Mind.* This volition, or power to act, is implanted in all forms of life, but comes to its highest fruition in the human mind. It is the *urge* of which I have already spoken, leading always to movement and to activity.

The Universe is a visible manifestation of the *Desire* of the *Supreme Intelligence*. Man as a microcosm or miniature reproduction of the Universal Prototype is an indigitation representing *individualized desire;* furthermore every man has a dominant and peculiar desire which distinguishes him from all other men. Still further, it is easily to be seen that every man is a bundle of many and various desires, some of them confused and conflicting, others clear and readily perceived; but in their entirety constituting practically all of his personal life. Thus *Desire* is the determining element back of all predispositions and personal tendencies, all character, personality and "temperament."

Life as it is lived is an unending struggle to satisfy a "want." This want takes on multitudinous forms, and drives us constantly in an endeavour to fulfil an insatiable and eternal desire. This inward craving for fulfilment is met by a *consciousness of the power to act;* and it is this which constitutes Will.

Thus we naturally associate will-power with an active or vital person, one who can bring to bear upon any problem a *moving power* sufficient to consummate and achieve it.

Will is the point of ignition, as it were, at which the potential energies of the soul are liberated and converted into active dynamic power. It is man's greatest tool for accomplishment. All other of his attributes are subservient to it.

The general unawareness of man of his true unity with Nature has condemned him for ages to a belief in the dominance of the superior elements of the Universe rather than in himself. It is as though an invisible director were always pulling wires from behind the scenes and making him act like a puppet. And until he awakens to a greater sense of his own capacity, he will be doomed to his old belief in "Fate" or "Providence" as a force before which he is destined to bow in acknowledgment of his own futility. This same universal power is often personalized as a God, who must be propitiated and conciliated in an endeavour to bend His Will if possible in some mysterious way to ours.

Even when Fate is designated as Nature, Principle, or First Cause, it has been regarded as a thing apart from man, and as being hopelessly, impersonally implacable and cold. Sometimes too, it has been called a Devil, since aught else, devised but to thwart and frustrate. "Inherited tendencies" have also been called in to account for this mysterious worker which seems so often to defy our Will; and some people, born apparently to create opposition, are reduced to the simple ignominy of declaring that "the whole world is against them."

In these various ways has man expressed his blind recognition of the existence of some *law*, some force which was bigger than he, and against which he seems to be for ever struggling; and always he has managed to put himself mostly at cross purposes with this great undercurrent, this transcendent Will, which I prefer to call Desire. As for the *word* Desire, he has dragged it in the dust and spat upon it as though to challenge with his disapproval this supreme force of the Universe.

When however, man comes to understand his relation to all the cosmic energies, as he is now beginning to, he will no longer feel that sense of separateness, which has driven him to *supplication* as the only means known to him for the fulfilment of his desires. He will know himself rather as a part of Fate itself, he will discover his personal Will to be one of the greatest channels of expression for the Divine Will. His conception of himself will be raised accordingly, he will become aware of his power.

Perhaps man's evolution has been possible only through this long combat, but for those who have the intelligence to see, there is a better and happier way than that imposed upon us by constant and painful resistance. There is in truth such a thing as *Free Will*. It lies in the simple recognition by man himself of his oneness with the Universal Will and hence a belief in the power and supremacy of his own. The question is not, as Locke said long ago, whether the *Will* be free but whether the *man* be free. My conception of the Superman is that his foremost attribute will be an understanding of the law of Freedom, thus making his Will paramount.

I well know the opposition that this attitude toward life arouses in many, especially those whose lives are cramped and bound. It strikes nothing less than terror to the hearts of those who have been taught to look upon man as a worm of the dust, and disconcerts the gentle souls who see in it only irreverence and sedition.

That it endows us with a majesty and Will to which we have long been accustomed is no reason for fear or hesitancy in using the forces of nature of which we are now obtaining a knowledge. "Fate is unpenetrated causes," says Emerson—"he who sees through the design presides over it and must Will that which must be"—"Will is poured into the souls of all men as the soul itself which constitutes them men."

Therefore we have but to realize the *fatefulness* of our own Wills to become true masters, the makers of our own destiny.

That this mighty precept cannot be applied without thought, intelligence, or a sense of values, especially spiritual values, I think is self-evident. The vital truth that man's Will is in its essential nature limitless, has been made unseemly by those of ready tongue, who with no foundation or qualification for the statement, unequivocally declare—"You can have all you want, you only need to want it hard enough." I suppose every great teaching has been reflected in some degraded form by the thoughtless and uninitiated; but I can conceive of nothing more shallow or foolish than to urge us to seek hastily, without knowledge of the psychology of desire, without consideration even of Law and Order, Truth and Fitness, to seize upon that which we "want," if we can. Depth of thought and sobriety of action are more required in this matter of Will than in any other department of human activity, for it brings in the whole moral question of *Duty,* or the recognition of the rights of others, as well as a knowledge of our own capacity.

The charge is often made, and rightly so, that much of the popular teaching regarding the human Will is distinctly unethical, in that it encourages the rank selfishness of a world already overridden with selfishness. This is no doubt true, but there is a clear distinction to be made between this spurious imitation, and the truth concerning the divinity of desire, or the right and potent use of our Wills.

If the latter leads to selfishness, it is but the Higher Selfishness which makes us stronger and more useful in every way, for from this vantage point we do not and cannot make the mistake of trying to impinge our own Wills and opinions upon others. The wise man demands freedom but knows that it cannot be acquired unless he gives in kind; and also he looks upon life from the esoteric rather than the exoteric point of view, seeing the inner meaning and valuing the things of mind and soul above those of place, power, or position. He knows that material things can be acquired or pre-

eminence gained, through an application of his
Will, but he also knows the dangers and futili-
ties involved in seeking these things for themselves alone, and in striving to advance himself
at the expense of others. He knows too that
often enough the Universal Will is overwhelming, as in this present world-war which is upon
us. Not that a Supreme Being has decreed it
so but that the totality of human Thought and
Will has expressed itself in this disastrous and
overwhelming way.

The problem is for each one of us to find our
own little orbit of action, and when found, to
bring a determinism to bear upon it in such a
way that it becomes, as nearly as may be, a
perfect life-unit. Few of us ever see our lives
in this detached manner, few of us ever believe
that we can master circumstances enough to
earn the coveted freedom.

Our ordinary life is made up of actions that
are largely automatic, habits and conventions
that form a crust around our free expression;
and it is only occasionally that we seem to
burst through this crust and express our whole

selves. It is not always that free action is
called for; but the test of it and the secret of
acquiring it, lies in a *unified personality*. It is
only when our acts spring from our *whole*
selves that they may be said to express free-
will. This is not only free-will in the mere
sense of choice, that is, the ability to select between two or more paths of action, but it means
also real *creativeness* and an irresistible driving power that *puts things through*.

There have been many philosophers and
thinkers to deny the freedom of the Will—it
is one of the oldest questions of the world and
it is not yet settled; but those who have de-
clared that independence of action was futile
and in the end always defeated, have not reck-
oned with the constantly unfolding spiritual
powers in man—such a view clips his wings at
the outset by teaching him that he can never fly.

We have only to look about us to see how im-
perious a man's Will may be—we have only to
compare lives of inefficiency and failure with
those where every obstacle, no matter how in-
surmountable it seemed, was met and overcome

by means of a mighty force within. How many
times do we see a life cast in the moulds of pov-
erty, ill health, disloyal friends, or unscrupu-
lous enemies, a life without position, place or
power in the world, but possessed of a *Will*
which chooses its own way and makes that way
unaided, simply by liberating the force enfolded in unquenchable desire, a force which in
time dissolves every obstacle and surmounts
all impediments.

Still, what is surprising to most people is
to discover that *we never do anything that we
have not willed to do;* not consciously willed of
course, for the deeper phases of Will, always at
work in the lower levels of consciousness, are
those which usually determine our actions.
This invisible element in the Will is the disconcerting one, for it is very often in direct opposition to the views and purposes of the conscious
self. It is the reason of the self-frustration
that causes so much trouble and makes us feel
that we are the victims of fate. The truth is
that the restraint lies not *without* but *within,*
and unless the enemy within the gates is *extir-*

pated or *reconciled,* life remains that which it usually appears to be, an endless friction and strife, leading only to the despairing and hopeless question of "what is the use"?

Our pet belief is that we are being constantly forced by circumstances into various avenues of action, all "against our will." Never was there a greater delusion, for if we submit to an external restraint of any kind, it is because we *prefer* it to the combat necessary to gain our freedom.

So many lives are made up of the breathless sort of feeling that comes from constant opposition and from the being obliged to do almost everything that they do not want to do. Yet the fact remains and on closer inspection will be seen to be always true, that somewhere within the depths of our own make-up, there is always a thread of Desire, a purpose, an impulse, that is solely responsible for our doing everything—even the very things we were apparently resisting with all our might. It is the resistance of our own unconscious desires that causes most of the mischief and forces us to remain in conditions we dislike and resent. It is these same desires which compel us in directions we never thought or dreamed of. And it is nothing more or less than our own personal Will, encrusted with all its limitations, which keeps us just where we are and which determines every act of our lives.

As it is Unconscious Will that accounts so largely for the variability of man's behaviour, it behooves us to remedy our ignorance, so far as we may, of what goes on below the surface. Even a cursory inspection reveals the fact that we are made up of a bundle of crisscross threads and impulses and desires, so conflicting in their nature that the wonder is that we ever make a single forward unified movement. We hardly know our own minds at all, being the repositories, as we are, of innumerable inherited impulses, and, to some extent, of all the Wills of all the other human beings with whom we in any way come in contact.

A brief study of mob psychology is proof, if such were needed, of the inability of the average human being to protect himself from the

Wills of those about him. When these coalesce, as they always do, more or less, especially under the strain of any emotional excitement, they present a force that is practically irresistible. In a way it is mob psychology that governs us all still and it requires a definite and conscious effort to raise one's self from out the slough that is made up of one part "influence" and the other part "susceptibility."

While the Will constitutes the very citadel of our being, it is constantly assaulted because of the extremely volatile quality of human nature, which furnishes the chief cause of division and weakness at the very source and origin of all our activities. By volatile, I mean that excessive susceptibility that comes of our belonging largely, as yet, to the *group consciousness*. Hawthorne expresses this very effectively somewhere in the "Scarlet Letter." He says, "It is anything but agreeable to be haunted by a suspicion that one's intellect is *exhaling*, without one's consciousness, like ether out of a phial; so that, at every glance, you find a smaller . . . residuum." Yet this is what is happening to most of us, practically all of the time. We are permitting ourselves to be *dispersed* instead of maintaining the necessary *integration.*

The progress of humanity is toward *individualization,* which means a recognition by the individual of his own power and right to power. This represents a degree of *self*-consciousness attained only by the few (as Will has hitherto been largely a blind force), but it is not beyond the reach of any.

My first prescription therefore for a "strong Will" is an *independent* and *self-confident attitude* as being the best means to lift us out of the group consciousness or race-thought, into one of our own making. We are much too much influenced by outside things—especially by our family, friends, the community and nation. We do not know what we think or what we want, because our habit has been to move only in established directions. The paths in the brain are mostly deep ruts worn there by long use, sustained by reverence for custom and tradition.

This prevailing attitude has an intimate relation to what is called a "weak will." Inherently every one is the possessor of a Will, else
he would not be self-existent, to say nothing of
self-sustaining. The weakness to be observed
on all sides is the result, not of inherent
lack of strength, but of a *division,* due to too
much obeisance to that which is without and
not enough recognition of that which is within.
The consequence is *indecisiveness,* than which
there is no more fundamental defect. Even a
slight degree of indecision disorganizes and
neutralizes the force of the Will as nothing else
can, and our aim should be to always act de-
cisively even in the trivial things of life, rather
than weigh and balance conditions until our
original force is diminished or expended.

To ask the average person what he really
wants is to throw him into a state of confusion
in which he flounders indefinitely before he is
able to catch upon even one thread that will
hold him. All are desirous of changing and
bettering their conditions in one way or another, but few realize that their failure to

achieve this progress is due more to an inability to clearly determine what they want and to abide by that determination, than to any other one factor. Even when recognized, the want takes the form of *wishing* rather than *willing*, which is a purely negative form and accomplishes nothing.

Will to be effective must therefore be *positive, concentrated, and unified.* The force of it is dependent upon the intensity of the desire behind it, and the elimination, or subjection at least, of every other conflicting desire. It is remarkable that so many people are unable to co-ordinate their various desires enough to centralize them into one general purpose. The power of the strongest current of water can be nullified, for instance, when it is met by an obstacle sufficient to turn its concentrated volume into a spray of multitudinous and separate drops. Many persons with the finest natural equipment are thus hopelessly weakened by an inability to throw into one steady stream their various impulses and purposes.

The common expression "to make a point of"

doing something indicates very well the mental operation that must prevail where success is to be achieved. We must "make a point of," that is *converge,* the conflicting elements in our natures until the full weight of them can for the time being be put upon a single point. Only thus is sufficient power generated to make a forward movement worth anything. Where so many fail is that the force of their Will is diffused over innumerable interests and half formed impulses, until its entire potentiality is dispersed and lost.

To be successful then in the use of the Will requires a very intimate relation between it and the selective discriminating quality of the *Intellect,* which we have already considered. It also means *sacrifice,* in that no human life is strong enough or long enough to satisfy *every* potential desire that springs up within it. Something must be eliminated, something selected, a singleness of purpose developed to secure anything like a full fruition of its power.

There is a very common habit, especially characteristic of Americans, of always "doing" something, with comparatively little or no direction. It is the result no doubt of an intense wish to "get on," admirable enough in itself, but detrimental in the extreme unless properly balanced and controlled. The ideal of our present civilization seems to be *emulation,* a desire to excel at any cost in almost every field of endeavour. Compared to the dreamy passivity of the Oriental, it may be regarded as a virtue, but as a nation we are overbalanced in our admiration for "will-power" *per se,* with a comparatively small consideration of the goal toward which we may be aiming. More thought should be given to the *purpose* of our actions, which would abrogate many of them entirely, and make the chosen ones more effective.

This whole question of being too susceptible to outside influences may be summed up as representing a *negative* state of mind. *Negativity,* psychologically speaking, is a state of mental passivity—not necessarily weakness, but frequently leading to weakness because it lacks resistance.

There are certain natures which may be said to be "negative" in their general quality, not lacking in beauty or attractiveness for this reason, but usually deficient in that projecting power or aggressiveness which is the expression of a normally active Will. Such people are frequently more agreeable companions than the more active ones and are attractive because of their very restfulness; just as we may sometimes prefer looking at the modest hare-bell rather than the flaming poppy. Very often, too, this passive manner and attitude is but external, and conceals a character much less yielding than it appears, though as a rule it is a sign of dangerous *negativity.*

Those born with a sweet and sympathetic disposition, given to retiring into the background when any more positive personality chooses to assert itself, suffer not so much from a weak Will, as from a form of sensitiveness which becomes positively harmful because of its inhibitory action upon their own natural impulses. The fact that this nature may be fine, or even of exquisite quality, and that it is usually an unselfish one, does not prevent it from entertaining too much respect and consideration for others to properly exercise its own rights and desires. It may even become, and often does, a regular door-mat, to be imposed upon and walked over by every stronger nature in its vicinity—a disastrous phase of *negativity,* needless to say.

As a Psycho-therapist and adviser to the sick and distressed, it has fallen within my province to bolster up a wavering self-confidence and to encourage more positive and ruthless attitudes than could well be believed by those less experienced in the pains and perplexities of a suffering humanity. Strange as it may seem, *negativity* prevails far more than its opposite, a positive egotism. Every one has his vulnerable spot or weakness, the point where his resistance melts away and breaks down. No doubt this is fortunate in a world yet governed by selfishness and greed—nevertheless, I must urge upon my readers the cultivation of that positive state of mind that knows no self-distrust, no uncertainty, no quiescence.

Perhaps one of the most desirable natures to
have is that which hides an iron hand beneath a
velvet glove—a simile that represents, though
crudely, the right balance that should be maintained between the negative and positive mental states.

Even those possessed of a reasonably active
and positive Will are often caught in the en-
tangling mesh of "following the line of least
resistance." Unfortunately for those who love
ease, the easiest way is seldom the best way.
It means sliding rather than propelling, going
with the current rather than creating a current for one's self. Great are the delusions
that people create for themselves to hide the
fact that they are not willing to make a fight,
exert the necessary amount of resistance to
overcome the various circumstances which arise
as obstacles in their path.

To follow the line of least resistance is indeed simply following an opposite *attraction*
of some sort; it pleases them better, though
they may not think so, to continue floating
along the stream of circumstance than to

buckle down and do some hard rowing. It is sheer mental laziness, a general dislike for exertion, a hatred of disturbance, and it leads to a damaging procrastination, if not to complete frustration and loss. It is one of the most insidious as well as common forms of the negative state of mind, and it can be eradicated only by earnest determined practice, a discipline that allows no slips, no variations in its self-imposed rigour.

Closely allied to the generally negative trend of most minds, is the paralyzing force of *Habit*. Habit in itself is constructive enough, indeed absolutely essential in that it enables us to turn over to the subconsciousness the doing of innumerable things which would be painfully laborious did they not so easily become automatic. Habit, however, like everything else must be properly balanced to be useful and many of us are standing helplessly on the negative side of this mental attribute. We are "staying put" with a vengeance, remaining bound by customs the usefulness of which we have long since outgrown.

The amazing number of early inhibitions which are uncovered by present psycho-analytic methods, serves as a sufficient warning to the wise of the habitual attitude. How many people are doing foolish things because they never thought of doing them any other way. How many refrain from new lines of action just because "it isn't done." How many of the precepts acquired in childhood have been *bête noires* which we dare not attack.

Nothing is so inhibitory to the development of new ideas as Habit. It is so much easier to go on in the old grooves than it is to carve out new ones; but who of us would not rather have the initiative to blaze a new trail than to follow unresistingly in the old ones? To be successful in the use of the Will signifies somewhat of iconoclasm. One must dare to be a breaker of idols would he give evidence of his divine origins.

We have already considered that phase of negativity which inclines to bow before the opinions and force of others, thus causing a division within the self; we have now to consider

another and even more important phase of it
which has to do with that inner conflict personal
to each human being, that battle and separation within himself which is an inevitable source
of trouble and weakness until the all important
lesson of self-mastery has been learned. I
have already touched upon this in my reference to the necessity for personal discipline, and
I shall consider still more fully in the succeeding chapter the nature and significance of *Emotion* as a driving force in human nature, and as
the greatest obstacle to the supremacy of Intellect and conscious Will. I wish here simply
to call attention to the dominance of unreasoning *Feeling* as the worst enemy of the free use
of the Will, and show that the autonomy of the
Self must be cultivated as against momentary
propensions and blind desires.

As a matter of fact, action is usually determined by the *phase* of the personality upper-
most at the moment. It is not chance or caprice in the sense of an external force or fate,
but some one of the many complex elements
in the mind emerging for the time being, which

takes the reins and drives us whither it wills. H. G. Wells says in one of his books: "It is just as though we were each of us not one person but many persons, who sometimes meet and shout all together, and then disperse and forget and plot against each other." Actions of this kind are without objective other than that dictated by impulse, and are necessarily erratic and tangential. Naturally the outcome is but partially effective and usually falls far short of the mark intended.

In a sense this uncertainty in the utilization of the Will is providential, for the reason that man in his present undeveloped state is unable to use so dynamic a power in a consistently constructive manner. The number of requests a practising Psychologist receives, for instance, of knowledge of how to "influence others" and make some one do what he does not want to do, is disheartening. Such a projection of will-power is of course perfectly possible and evidences of its use on the psychic plane are numerous and easily verifiable; but they are not the lines of action that it is wise to give instruction in even when one knows something of the procedure, because of the very real danger in the psychic use of the Will, both to the operator and to his subject.

It is well, therefore, as I have just intimated, that the impelling force of the Will does not always secure its end; but I assume that my readers are interested, as I am, in a purely constructive development of the Will, and toward this end I can give many assurances of an increased personal power and efficiency by the eradication of internal dissension and the assertion of proper authority over the emotions.

A man is internally free only when the ends he pursues have his whole-hearted approval; but most of us start out to do things without much thought as to whether the accomplishment of those particular aims are what we most desire or not. If one really desires wealth, for instance, it can be acquired by sufficient concentration upon it; but to do this successfully requires sacrifice of many other occupations and interests, the loss of which may never be compensated for by the satisfaction of the desire to be rich. Thus a certain amount of deliberation should be one's habit before attempting to project one's force in any given direction. Much waste is occasioned by following false leads, leads that do not draw forth one's full quota of strength because they do not represent one's full desire.

We all know that the shortest distance between any two points is a straight line, and we should learn to utilize Will in this way, that is, by being so certain of our direction that there is no wavering. When once chosen, a plan should be adhered to without the slightest doubt or deviation, unless indeed all the original factors upon which one's decision was made should be changed. Otherwise there will be numerous conflicting desires which if they do not exactly oppose the original desire will probably succeed in negating its final consummation by reason of the variance implied.

A man thinks he wishes to change his business, for example, but feels that he is obliged to continue in it by force of circumstances. He does not realize that the phrase "by force of circumstances" implies another Will in himself than the one which would lead him to give up or change his business. His basic desire is to be engaged in some lucrative occupation, something that will earn his living, enable him to care for his family, *etc.;* but the conflict arises when the *form* of this occupation is to be determined. If he remains where he is, it is because he *prefers* it to the exertion of his Will that will be required to create new circumstances for himself; it is this preference which makes him continue with that which he declares he is not willing to continue.

In order to work upon a straight line in a situation like this, it is first well to deliberate upon the fundamental and general purpose— the desire to be active and successful. To be busy and even moderately successful is worth a great deal, so much, in fact, that the contemplation of it should remove for the most part the minor oppositions within one's self which tend to create friction. There is a still further constructive attitude, however, which would seek

to harmonize both the original desire and the
lesser one concerning the form which that desire should take. Few men are successful in
any line of endeavour that does not command
their spontaneous interest—in other words,
one should aim to unite his *liking* for certain
forms of activity with his need for a good living.

This is only one instance of many which will
suggest themselves to the mind of the thoughtful reader, as to the manner in which he should
handle his own desires. It should be his creed
to believe in them, to regard them as the only
sure guide posts to success; and where circumstances force a division of his interests, he
should make himself *like* even that, until he is
able to blend the opposing elements.

It is in order here to call attention to the fact
that *dislike* in any form is a negative state of
mind, although it often appears to be the contrary. It is negative because it represents a
"split" in one's self. We do not bother to dislike the things that do not concern us—we are
merely indifferent to them—and if we enter-

tain a feeling of opposition, it indicates two conflicting wishes within one's self which have not
been properly co-ordinated. Further, nothing
betrays the presence of an unconscious trend
in the opposite direction so much as a marked
strenuousness of conscious effort to overcome
or avoid it. The woman for instance, who is
frequent in her protestations that her husband
loves her is but thus expressing her unconscious
fear that he does not. *"Qui s'excuse s'accuse."*

Where Intellect and Emotion are properly
balanced, Will has the best possible opportunity for free expression. We all know the difficulty of exercising the Will *against* the motive
power that is supplied by Desire. Even in the
simple matter of going for a walk one may find
it very fatiguing to insist on the necessary mus-
cular activity, whereas when the attention is
distracted by means of pleasant company, the
effort or feeling of resistance is quite removed.
So, would we have our behaviour harmonious
and forceful, we must utilize the impelling
power of Emotion where we can; but at the
same time we must learn to draw very clearly

that line of demarcation where Feeling assumes the dominant rôle, subjugating the Will into a pitiful insignificance.

Perhaps in no place is this frequent occurrence more noticeable than in the dominance of physical sensations. The common tendency to pet and pamper various bodily symptoms is but an evidence of the ascendancy of Feeling over Will. Whereas one person will be prostrated by a pain, another with the same annoyance will preserve his poise and mastery, thus shortening by many minutes or years, as the case may be, the disturbing experience. The extreme susceptibility of many patients to various meteorological conditions, changes in temperature, clothing, surroundings, food, and sleep, but indicate how dormant is the Will and how exalted is Sensation.

The tendency to self-indulgence does not confine itself only to physical habits, but spreads through the entire emotional and psychic life. It is a marvellous endowment to be able to *feel,* to be so sensitized as to register all grades and forms of sensation; but nothing is more weakening or injurious than to allow this faculty complete sway without holding the Will in its position of authority, where it may temper and control as it can and should.

With many years' experience as a Psychotherapist as the basis of my opinion, I find no human attribute in greater need of development than that of the Will. A large number of definite physical diseases can be entirely overcome by a proper re-education of the subconscious Will; and even those that are more complicated psychologically, still require the discipline that leads to self-mastery, especially the mastery of the *feelings*.

There are those of course, whose insistence on the use of their Will is excessive and who suffer accordingly a dearth of ease, spontaneity, and natural feeling. There is such a thing as *trying* too hard and as a habit it becomes detrimental in that it creates *tension* and develops a "hot box" somewhere in the system, either physically or mentally.

Many disease reactions arise out of this state of mind and many are the disappointments also that await those who do not know the balancing law of *non-resistance*. Where to draw the line between an unswerving determinism and an easy adaptable non-resistance that has in it somewhat of the quality of unconcern— this is a problem that cannot be solved by one for another. By experience, however, one eventually learns the joy of *effortless activity*.

"How to develop the Will" is one of those catch phrases of modern days so well illustrative of our desire to "get on" and extract the juice of life in the quickest way possible without much question as to whether we are really satisfying our hunger. The charlatan, or even the sincere but poorly informed psychologist, does not require unusual enterprise to attract public attention to his wares, if he but utter the magic phrase "how to develop the Will."

The extensive but ill-assorted modern literature on the subject of the Will centres almost wholly about this phrase, and while some of it is rich in suggestion and not infrequently contains evidences of genuine effort to be helpful, it is as a rule so lacking in any understanding of the true nature of the subject as to be practically useless. It is like trying to run a motorcar without any knowledge of the engine or its construction, so that the first obstacle met with on the road is more than apt to cause a breakdown.

Having examined somewhat of the principle and origin of Will power, we know that any efforts to develop it with success must be based on a knowledge of its complexities and its relation to the whole mind of which it is so integral a part.

To bring forth any act of the Will in its completion, there are, as I conceive it, three steps which are quite readily distinguishable.

a. *Concept*
b. *Intention*
c. *Execution.*

The first of these, *"Concept,"* is really a creation of the Imagination, a forming in the mind of an Idea; a recognition of Concept, or Ideation, is the first step in any act of the Will.

The second, *"Intention,"* is an expression of *Desire.* It supplies motive-power for the mental image, thus vitalizing the *Concept* to the point of definite form—the second step in any act of the Will.

The third, *"Execution,"* represents that crisp finishing quality which brings things forth from the inner world into outer manifestation, and is the consummation of any act of the Will.

These three elements must be properly combined and related for Will to be effective. We can see about us at any time and in the acts of most people, evidences of some one of these phases separated from its proper sequence—the result being equivalent to a dog trying to walk on three legs when he was meant to use four.

Let us take the phase of *Concept* alone. Many people are teeming with ideas and mental images, producing more concepts than they know what to do with. The result is a mass of undigested material floating around vaguely in their minds, their creators quite unable to formulate anything clearly enough to bring either intention or execution to bear upon it. Inventors, notably prolific in their creation of

ideas, are equally notable for their impractical-
ity—their inability to "bring down to earth"
the concepts which crowd their brains. There
are others besides "inventors" too, who fall
within this class! Dreamers we call them and
we may love them, but how we do wish that
they might bring their thinking forth into the
objective world, rather than waste so much of
it in the realm of fancy.

There are also those who are for all practical
purposes devoid of ideas, who lack the imaging, apprehending faculty to such an extent
that they are without any premise from which
to make a move. They cannot *intend* anything, because of the vagueness and generally
nebulous quality of all their thinking. With
either too many or too few "ideas," one is
liable to failure.

Probably the most frequent of all is the type
of person who is full of *intentions,* whose concepts are fairly clear and who "means" to
utilize them all, but who yet lacks the *Will* to
execute any of his various notions. We all
know the name of the place to which this road

leads. Nothing is more self-deluding than to carry about a lot of perfectly good intentions without materializing them. He who gives a promise lightly without *intention* or thought of the labour entailed to consummate it, is the cause not only of many unhappy hours to his family and friends, but injures himself past redemption through falling into a habit of sheer futility. The discrepancy between *Intention* and *Execution* marks man's greatest weakness and his behaviour is more hampered by this limitation of mental abortiveness than by any other thing.

Intentions that bear fruit mark the person possessed of executive ability and are characteristic of all those who occupy high places. If one made a habit of finishing all the things that one begins, even in the details, it would not be long before the power of bringing to a successful close any project, on however large a scale, would be not only possible but habitual.

A type of which we see much in these days however, is one in which "Execution" is developed to a high degree without a correspond-

ing balance in the other two phases of the Will
—it becomes a mere case of "doing" without
respect to quality or purpose. Such a one is
always "executing" something, his ideas are
literally "done to death" by his overwhelming
desire to be active, to bring to pass, willy nilly.
He hurries from place to place, he is for ever
busy and he frequently does get things done;
but what it is that he is getting done never
troubles him. He lacks plan and purpose, has
no clear conception or even intentions; or possibly has such a multiplicity of both that he
never has time to follow them out and thus
utilize to some advantage his capacity for execution. We speak of a musical person as possessing good execution when he has facility
without the soul or spirit of the composition he
should be endeavouring to interpret. Mere activity is the outermost rim of the circle represented by Will, a hollow hoop without the cen-
tralizing and spiritual quality which constitutes
its very essence.

We are, of course, using our Wills every day
and all the time, but between the uncertainty

with which we use them and the superficiality that prevails, it is small wonder that we so seldom attain our true ends.   To sum up the ethical as well as the practical import of a study of Will, I should first say that we need above all to cultivate an *affirmative attitude;* secondly that we should search much more deeply for our springs of action than we have been accustomed to.

Emerson's magnificent statement "I *am,* therefore, I *can*" should help us in the first. To live with such a maxim in the foreground of one's consciousness, is to develop those settled principles and consistent policies which alone lead to lasting achievement.   The *Opportunist* is one without fixed purpose or reasoned action, he usually "tries to do his best" under the circumstances, but fails because his action is all pendent upon externalities.   He takes "circumstances" as his premise rather than the sure granite of his own Will.   *Determination* is the equivalent of *Causation* in the physical world. Man is his own unfailing source—if he but knew it.

The second important element to master in
the Will is the power of the Unconscious. Here
we have a host of impulses, most of them
primal, crude, unshaped, and powerful. Desire, which is behind all Will, represents a whole
strata of instinctive feelings which are in themselves a force so great as to prove irresistible
more often than not. These tendencies are
Will in its most fundamental aspect, Will in-
spired by the great natural motive-power of
Feeling. Our whole progress hangs upon the
guidance through the Intellect of *unconscious*
Will—it does not imply the suppression of Emotion, but the proper *placing* of it in relation to
purpose and *Intention*.

It is necessary also to place a new value on
Desire. Desire in its true sense is frequently
very dormant, latent, lost in the depths of the
subconsciousness, and the cultivation of it is a
department of human activity by itself. Every
one who finds himself weak on this score, inclined to indifference or unconcern, would do
well to listen as with his ear to the ground, for
those under-currents of feeling in himself, those

cravings which represent the purpose and direction of his being. One of our great modern publicists, David Jayne Hill, says—"The great problem of society is to release the free activity of human faculties." This is indeed the problem of society and also the problem of the individual. If our schools were what they should be, instructors in the great problems of the mental and moral life, the first and last lessons would be concerned with the development and control of the human Will.

CHAPTER V

EMOTION

THE PSYCHOLOGY OF FEELING

EMOTION, the mainspring of all Behaviour and the human expression of *Feeling* or responsiveness to life, is the first and most primitive phase of cognition or self-consciousness, the most definitely recognizable of all the psychic states. Because primitive it is powerful—that is, primitive in the sense of being essential and original, not superadded, complex, or developed, as is the Intellect. *Instincts,* man's simplest feelings, represent his very first reactions to his environment, and as *Emotion* implies a conscious *recognition* of this feeling-state it may be said to mark the beginnings of self-consciousness.

Both in development of the race and of the individual, *Feeling* always precedes Thought. In animals we call it *Instinct.* In his early

191

stages of development, *Instinct* prevails in man also, even as it does in the child, and it is only with the growth of the *Intellect* that we have what may be properly called *Emotion*.

Instincts, belonging as they do to the more primitive phases of existence, have come to be associated more especially with physiological needs and processes.   *Emotions* are essentially psychological in their nature, because they appear only in those stages of development where an unfolding Intellect has made it possible to apprehend or be aware of our inherited instinctive forces and reactions.   We do not, therefore, say of animals that they have *Emotions,* although we know that they do possess *feelings.* Carrying this distinction further, all man's unconscious feelings would be *Instincts* and all his conscious feelings *Emotions;* but as it is impossible for obvious reasons to make such a division exact, I shall use the terms in a somewhat looser sense, with reference to their various inter-relations.

The baby begins by *feeling* his way through life.   In Feeling he evinces his first power of response to his environment. He *feels* not only physically, but psychically as well, and his reaction to his surroundings is for a long time wholly dependent upon his power to thus apprehend the external world. With the development of the Intellect the feeling phase of consciousness subsides to some extent, though still active in the subconsciousness; and though neither the child nor primitive man is *aware* of the function of feeling, he is completely dominated by it until such time as the Intellect may, after a long and uncertain battle, gain its ascendancy.

The child or the immature man is therefore apt to be "impulsive," that is, he responds quickly and unconsciously to his own various psychic states and translates them into action without forethought or question—a necessary mode of development in the earlier stages and one not to be too quickly supplanted by more intellectual methods at any time.

Yet civilization represents our effort as a whole to become aware of our various Feelings and learn to master them. Nature's blind forces, always silently and potently at work, are constantly clashing with the growing force of Intellect. The whole of man's progress is marked by the development of the seeds of self-consciousness, until by means of the Will, as we have seen, he rises to kingship in a realm where he has so long been the mere puppet of a blind fate. This combat is fundamental, never-ending, and frequently discouraging. The odds are great against us in the elemental domain of the Emotions, though not too great, as any sane and thoughtful person knows.

As though fearing our lack of control, we instinctively shrink from Feeling, *per se,* probably because it implies an *agitation.* The original meaning of the word Emotion was *commotion,* and our appreciation of this its real significance, leads us to seek refuge very often in the calmer states where Intellect alone prevails. Also, with the development of the refinements and discriminations of civilization, many of our original feelings, especially the instincts, become unseemly, too animal-like, to pass the approval of our higher natures and we thus wish to repress them.

Granting all this, it must be admitted for the proper contrast and balance, that we have also *lost* much, since this original and primitive form of response to life has become so overlaid with intellectual conceptions. Whether it be through fear of a force not yet understood and conquered, or whether to the emasculating influence of purely intellectual refinements, the fact remains that the essential power and value of Feeling has been reduced to a minimum that is distinctly detrimental to the harmony and strength of life as a whole.

All education tends to deprecate any *display* of Emotion; we have even reached the point where to conceal it entirely is considered as a mark of the highest culture. This alone implies our false estimate of its value and leads to its further diminution or extinction; and in the meantime we are left at the mercy of a force which knows no mercy—we have merely repressed and checked—we have *not* mastered.

The path leading toward the ultimate supremacy of the Intellect and Will is, of course, as I
have already pointed out, both an important
and necessary one, for the reason that conscious
Intellect is the only qualifying agent for Emotion, and affords the guiding channel for a
power otherwise unrestrained and dangerous
in its intensity. But we have gone so far in the
worship of the controlling and inhibiting faculties, as to lose our perspective and essential
hold on some of the more vital things, without
really gaining the sovereignty we are aiming
for. We have succeeded only in *suppressing*
or *distorting* practically all of our natural impulses. Scarcely one of them flows forth without the restraining influence of social convention, public opinion, personal advantage, or
some other modifying agent, until we have completely deflected at its very source the mainspring and impulse of all human behaviour.
We have seen how the infant leads a subjective
and natural existence, but we have failed to
notice that in the subsequent development of
the conscious controlling faculties, the original

foundation has been much tampered with and in many instances wholly disorganized.

We forget the tremendous potentiality that lies concealed in our capacity to Feel. All through life it affords a far wider scope and a deeper revelation than the Intellect. It implies, indeed, nothing less than the whole realm of the Unconscious with all the delicate apprehensions of its Intuition.

Though less discriminating Feeling is far more subtle and penetrating because of its very subjectivity; and because it is capable of taking us into the deeps of experience and touching the divine fires, we recoil in trepidation, afraid, perhaps, to approach those elements of unalloyed power.

What is *enthusiasm,* for instance, but an intense capacity to *feel,* and what is there to be found of strength in the cold passionless survey of life afforded by the Intellect, unless it is vitalized by the Emotions? How far can Intellect carry one in an appreciation of nature, beauty, music, and all the warm human relationships such as love, reverence, and sympa-

thy? These are the things we *feel,* and while
the *explanations* afforded by the Intellect are
both useful and interesting, how paltry and insignificant they appear by the side of the actual
experience and realization.

It is like standing outside of a beautiful
palace, vainly trying to describe by means of
words the wonderful possessions it contains—
one must enter and see and feel for himself,
in order to know or appreciate its contents.
And so it is with life, we must first experience or feel, afterward we can take the
detached view afforded by the Intellect and
draw what conclusions Reason dictates.

The problem then, manifestly, is to find the
balance between Emotional Power on the one
side and Will Power and Intellect on the other.
In the first case, we have the whole gamut of
human feeling from its most savage primitive
instincts up to its highest aspirations and sympathies.

The greater the power, the greater the haz-
ard in the possession of it. Man's highest capacity lies in his sensitiveness to Feeling, but

in it also is enfolded his bitterest enemy and his greatest liability to error. Fortunately in the Will he has the right commanding and restraining influence, which can check, co-ordinate, and encourage wherever required for his best interests. It must of course be properly aligned with the Intellect and stand in the forefront as would a general leading an army, if the eternal combat is to be solved.

In order to throw some light upon this baffling problem of the control of the Emotions, and to enable earnest students of Psychology to so determine their own behaviour that it shall always be constructive, a close study of the action and reaction of the many and complex human impulses is most necessary.

In the first place, it is possible to make two general classifications, which though very broad in their nature, assist materially in reducing to its elements this appallingly complicated task. They are the simple ones that we have already observed in some of the previous studies—*i.e.*, that of *negative* and *positive*. With a little research and experience it is possible to place all Emotions clearly in one or the other of these divisions.

Under *Negative Emotions* I have classed all those attributes requiring *Control* or the interference of the Will; and under *Positive Emotions,* are all such as need to be encouraged or developed to make for a strong and rounded character.

It might be thought at first glance that this classification would be the old familiar one of *Vice* and *Virtue,* but such is not the case, especially if one is to regard human motives, as one should, from a purely dispassionate and un-moral point of view. Most works on ethical Psychology make the error of cataloging certain of our traits and tendencies as ''good,'' and the others as ''bad.'' In truth there is no such distinction whatever, as all the discord and pain and so-called evil in life rises solely out of a lack of proportion and proper relativity. There is no Emotion which in its essential nature can be called bad; but all of them, even the best, may be so misplaced or ill-used as to become, in effect, the worst. Of the *Negative Emotions* I mention four primary ones—

Fear

Anger

Grief

Self-love

The first of these, *Fear,* has the widest ramifications and is the most destructive of them all. The usual conception of Fear is one associating it exclusively with physical cowardice, but it requires only a moment's thought to perceive the fallacy of this view, for Fear has many forms and in one way or another is so prevalent as to honeycomb the whole fabric of the emotional life.

In its positive and constructive form Fear is simply *caution* or *forethought,* a defensive conservative instinct and an attitude necessary as a protection against the uncertainties of life; but the more common and negative aspect of it is that of "worry." Fore-thought becomes fear-thought when it does not build or construct a way out of the difficulty—a mere worry, which consists in treading ceaselessly

in a circle, arriving nowhere. It expresses
nothing but *futility* and is the outcome of habitually regarding life and all its forces as an
enemy rather than a friend. Such a state of
mind is Fear in its very essence and implies in
oneself a lack of confidence or power to overcome.

That many diseases and physical breakdowns
are due directly to the worry habit is now a matter of common knowledge; though the medical
man with his material remedies has no way of
dealing with the mental cause of his patient's
weakened resistance. He may suggest a sea
voyage or change of scene in the hope that
this re-distribution of attention may divert the
mind of the patient from its destructive channels. In some cases such is sufficient to effect
a cure—more often, however, it is necessary to
directly attack the Fear or worry itself in order
to remove the depressing symptoms, this being
the essential task of the Psycho-therapist.

Many experiments have been made of late
years and articles written to prove the presence of toxic elements in the blood as the im-

mediate result of the fear-state; and the close relation between morbid mental states and the secreting glandular action of the body has also been demonstrated. There is in these facts alone, one would think, a sufficient deterring influence to restrain the constant tendency to indulge in fears and doubts; but their forms are insidious and numerous and their hold so strong as to paralyze the Will and becloud the Intellect of the average sufferer.

Among the most prevalent specific forms of the anxiety-habit is that of the *fear of disease* in itself, many illnesses being the direct outcome of it especially when it is strong enough to become an obsession or fixed idea. Often a particular disease, or even an accident, will be unconsciously selected as the bugbear to disturb the peace of one's mental household. Frequently the sufferer from a phobia of this kind has no knowledge of whence came his thoughts on the subject. Under proper analysis they usually can be uncovered and the bringing of them into daylight may be sufficient to release the "common sense" that has been inhibited thereby. Our part as students of Behaviour is to recognize these various mental states as pathological and to seek so far as we personally are concerned to avoid the entrance or fixation in our minds of any concepts based on Fear.

Next to a fear of disease, in its frequency and destructiveness, comes a *fear of failure,* a feeling directly related to the struggle for existence, especially the economic struggle and the desire to "get on" to which I have referred before. Much of this Fear is artificial because based on false standards. It is an expression of that overwhelming desire to "keep up appearances." It leads to show and pretence, in a vain effort to bolster up a nature lacking in self-confidence and independence.

Yet it is necessary to admit that this anxiety also has its positive side and being the outgrowth as it very often is of admirable ambition pitted against the complexities of modern civilization, we must have more patience and sympathy with it than with many of the other negative mental states. The main business of

life is to secure by one's own efforts that which
is necessary to live and grow by, and while this
often seems a most difficult thing to do, I firmly
believe that if less attention were bestowed
upon various external obstacles, such as the
economic conditions of the times, *etc.*, and
more upon the internal functions of Will and
Intellect, there would turn out to be enough for
everybody, with no very good basis for this
prevalent anxiety.

Nature is lavish, only man is niggardly, and
with the enlargement of his consciousness to
the inclusion of the higher elements of mind
and soul, he will no longer feel the pinch and
cramp of conditions—he will instead declare
his freedom and know that there is no such
thing as failure *except to those who believe in
it.* It is only a relative term anyway, and does
not exist for those whose faith in themselves
remains unimpaired.

Fear of opinion is another negative state that
absolutely determines the lives of most people.
I have already spoken of how few know the nature of their true desires, there are equally few

who know and live by their own opinions. So
subtle and so strong is the pressure of subconscious thought-currents that the majority do not
realize that most of their ideas have been made
for them by others and accepted at secondhand.

I should say too that there is quite as much
Fear of holding to one's own opinion as there
is of incurring the disfavour of others. How
often we are untrue to the deeper flashes of our
own consciousness is indicated by the fact that
at some later period, when perhaps a greater or
better known mind gives voice to our smothered
feelings, do we see that we were afraid to recognize our own mental offspring. "No one's else
opinion can be as good as mine—for me" should
be the creed of every man. And as for the opinions of others, why exalt them so? Beyond a
reasonable receptivity and desire to profit by
the findings of others we should have no room
for their opinions as such. As for collective
opinion, that known as convention, there are
times when it is fitting that one should bend to
it for the sake of peace or the good of the whole,
but to *live* by it is to be hampered in the soul.

It is only he who is fearless in both thought
and action who attains to any real happiness
or strength. Many are the cowards who having the intelligence to see what is just and
right, yet lack the courage to uphold their
views and by silence give consent to that which
in their hearts they disapprove.

As to the causes of Fear there are many;
inherited race-thoughts start us off with many
deeply imbedded superstitions and destructive
ideas in our subconsciousness of which we are
never aware until they break forth at some unexpected moment. There are fears galore
based upon our own past painful experiences
and those of our ancestors: and even more
that have no "facts" for their basis at
all; but probably the most prolific source
of all is that arising in early childhood, when
the exceedingly harmful methods employed
by most parents to gain the obedience of
their offspring leads them unwittingly into
marking for life the mind of a sensitive child
with some fear that would otherwise be quite
alien to his nature.

From the very beginning the child has a price placed upon his veracity, his kindliness, his sociability, his natural curiosity—in short, upon nearly all of his most useful instincts. The average parent does not hesitate to stoop to the most primitive and barbarous methods and customs in order to impress his authority upon his child. He threatens him with the vengeance of everything from the dog and the policeman up to his Creator. Thus the child's natural instinct of Fear, which might otherwise remain dormant until it was needed in self-protection, is fed on the vagaries and stupidities of his elders until it outweighs every other feeling in his little brain.

Having made a special study of the origin of the innumerable Fears with which the average adult is burdened, I have come to the conclusion that we are, in the care of our children, still in the dark ages of superstition—for we almost universally sentence these free young lives to an inescapable fate, by instilling into them in their tender years all our own weaknesses, and then adding thereunto some spe-

cially devised ones, as it were, to fit the inno-
cence of childhood.

An excellent exercise for any student of Behaviour is to have a quiet séance with himself
in which to make an honest list of all his Fears
—for to entertain even one means not only a
diminution of one's strength and resistance,
but also a loss of opportunity. Let him realize that all Fear is founded primarily on a
sense of inferiority and that if he would be rid
of the misery of anxiety, or a sense of defeat, he
must do so by changing the pivot or point
of balance between his own power and the
power with which he endows mere circumstance.

It means the use of the Will of course; and a
rousing of the deep forces of the Self. Once
this positive state is thoroughly established,
which it may be in any case by earnest practice, there is no place left for the fear-feeling
to assert itself—even the habit of "apprehensiveness" and the fear of Fear may be thus
overcome. The Imagination is of course productive of all sorts of disturbing images and
gives rise to forebodings based either on experi-

ence or on prospective situations which it builds up out of sheer contrariness and lack of control; but he who claims any mastery of his Emotions becomes likewise a master of his Imagination and bids it build only those images which in the end will enable him to cast out all Fear.

Next to Fear, *Anger* properly takes its place as the greatest influence on human behaviour. All the centuries of civilization have not been able to eradicate or even ameliorate to any extent this expression of the instinct to *fight;* which in most of its manifestations in civilized society would give better grounds than anything else for a belief in human depravity or "original sin." Yet, Anger is one of those primitive feelings designed to help us maintain our individuality and establish our place in life, and when expressed as "righteous indignation" there is nothing finer. It is manifestly a part of what is called the cruelty of nature, wherein every unit, every atom has some part to play and holds its own only by reason of friction and resistance.

We know the prevalence of this law in the animal and plant world; and how out of the eternal conflict there is always a "survival of the fittest." This action and reaction of each unit one against the other when manifested in the life of man, whose most primal instinct of all is self-protection, expresses itself naturally as combativeness or Anger. It is the *offensive* form of the conservative instinct, and the entire absence of it means either a flatness or a yielding quality in the make-up which is sure to be disastrous. There are many natures too *good* or too soft and sympathetic to be possessed of enough strength or aggression to bring these virtues into their rightful fruition. The person who is *incapable* of feeling indignation or Anger is incapable of meeting life with sufficient self-assertion to ever master its oppositions and its obstacles.

With the development of the race there has come gradually the development of the social instinct with its larger aspects of unselfishness and altruism, until today our *ideals* are those of community life and co-operation. Every life is now more or less protected by a common aim or sentiment, the instinct of "humanity," so that Anger in its cruder forms is confined mostly to the savage races. In tracing this development we can see how an instinct which is essentially protective in its nature, may become detrimental, both to its possessor and its object, if it be entertained to any extent.

Yet the power to resent an imposition and to protect one's own against assault, is necessary —we have not yet reached the point where any one individual is accorded his "rights" unless he evinces an ability to secure them on his own behalf.

Having thus drawn attention to the positive phases of Anger, I wish to dwell a little upon the weakness of its negative side which shows forth in many ways, such as resentment, irritability, animosity, and hatred. It is my firm belief that there is no place for any of these emotions in a well-regulated life.

As is the case with all the primitive instincts, Anger is the greatest possible drawback unless it is mastered and controlled. It always expresses an inner conflict of some kind and usually betrays a lack of poise and dignity, which does not speak well for the character of its possessor. There is the Anger which rises quickly and subsides almost as soon as it is born, which is really more of an escape valve than anything else, and for which its possessor is usually quickly forgiven; but even this display of temper is not agreeable or constructive and exhibits a weakness or vulnerability. So strong may the emotion of Anger become as to drive its victim into acts of the greatest violence, for which he is obliged to spend a lifetime of regret. Its presence shows strength of a kind, but also, because of the lack of control, a great weakness.

There are those who contend that it is necessary to be able to *hate*, as an evidence of strength. This is a foolish fallacy; for while admitting the necessity of the *potentiality*, there is no necessity whatever for such a degree of aggression, even on the mental plane. Hatred is an element equalled in its destructive power by almost no other human feeling—if man is anywhere to demonstrate his supremacy over the animal world it must be at this point, for hatred is the result of the power of the Intellect added to Anger.

One may *hate,* in the sense of disapprove, many of the obnoxious or offensive elements of life with all propriety, although *ignoring* is a much more effective weapon. But of real hatred the evil is unto the hater much more than the hated—an overmastering emotion with nought but poison in it.

Even the lesser forms of hatred such as quarrelsomeness, animosity and meanness are all a great wastage of human energy. They never by any chance do good and they are always certain to do harm. Where we see them active we may know without further examination that their possessor is low indeed in the scale of development spiritually.

Among the lighter aspects of Anger, *irritability* is perhaps the most common and annoying one. Those who habitually give vent to this Emotion are not only a great trial to their

companions but are really destructive agents
in that they are the active centres of disturbed
forces and thereby destroy much of the peace
and harmony of those about them.   Of course,
there is the old excuse of bad digestion, *etc.,* for
those afflicted with this unfortunate habit, but
if a close examination be made, it will usually
be found that the habit preceded the gastric
disturbance and nine times out of ten was the
cause of it.

Like every other peccadillo, irritability has
its pathological side.   Untold benefit has already accrued from the work of Psycho-ther-
apists and Psycho-analysts who have found in
various repressions and mental mal-adjust-
ments the hidden cause of an irritability that
was as unaccountable to its possessor as to his
friends.   Always a search should be made for
the ''sore spot'' in the mind—once found the
Anger can be removed or properly harmonized
with its constituent elements.

But a bad disposition is very often only an
expression of a self-indulgent nature, using
this unconscious means to call attention to it-

self. A *habit* of "grouchiness" is well-nigh inexcusable, betraying as it does a long harboured resentment of some kind. The feeling of pleasantness as well as that of exasperation, can be encouraged no matter what we may have to contend with, and is in itself a partial cure for the annoying circumstances whatever they may be.

As for bursts of temper, they are but external signs of some repressed and unassimilated force, usually where the creative life has been checked or hemmed in until it finds this destructive mode of relieving the pressure. They can be "cured" just as any other disease can be. Many cases have been overcome by a simple determination on the part of the victim to effect a change, but they also often require expert analysis to uncover their true cause. All parents should be well enough trained in this mode of observation to find the reason of bad temper in their children—more often than not they may find it in themselves!

Resentment, a feeling of annoyance for the failure of people or conditions to come up to

our own standards, is a form of Anger. Here
again I must counsel the non-resistant mental
attitude, for he who carries a resentment in his
heart knows not the law of personal freedom, he is binding himself by demanding that
of another which he has not seen fit, or is not
able, to give. The whole attitude is based on
a false conception of our claims upon others;
we really have no claims at all and in all personal relations at least, should be content to
accept that which is extended spontaneously,
asking or expecting nothing more. When
properly understood this spirit is perfectly
compatible with a righteous self-assertion,
which to be successful must be maintained without the slightest trace of Anger.

Nursing a Grievance is still another form of
Anger, often protracted into a subconscious
resentment lasting over a long period of time.
I thus know of one otherwise admirable woman
who has for many years nourished and suf-
fered from this destructive feeling all because
her husband's sister has never seen fit to call
upon her and welcome her as one of his fam-

ily.   Small or large as the cause may be, the emotion itself is strongly akin to revenge, only it is more negative being a combination of *hurt pride* with Anger.

So many useless and unnecessary forms of Anger prevail where there is an admixture, more or less, of blind self-love, or perhaps a feeling of having been overridden.   If one has been triumphed over by another Will it should be accepted gracefully with a quiet reservation to the effect that a new standard has been set for one's strength, a new reach required.   Instead of resenting the success of a more positive Will, or feeling "injured," one should seek to become equally as positive; or if inclined to be "argumentative," learn to relax and not "care."   Only thus can one remove the sting that comes from having been "hurt"—to be given to "feeling hurt" is a·negative form of Anger and avails one nothing—a recognition of it should be a sufficient incentive to arouse the Will to a more constructive action.

Selfishness, or self-love, is the primary root of all evil.   It is, in its way, as negative as

Fear, refuting as it does all the outgoing and expanding elements that distinguish human being as apart from animals. In spite of its appearance as a positive expression, we can easily perceive its utterly negative character when we realize how completely it is the denial of all that is progressive and constructive. It tends to destroy the whole fabric of human life by separating and tearing apart, exalting as it does oneself at the expense of others. It may show as avariciousness and soulless greed, or it may be only a carelessness of the comfort and happiness of others; but in all forms it is offensive because so completely obverse to all that is highest and best in life.

The deep and almost unconquerable influence of self-love is due to its inherently protective and conserving nature. There are people, for instance, who are not selfish enough for their own welfare, who lose the best of life by their readiness to be imposed upon by other stronger natures. Yet even selfishness can scarcely be said to exist *per se,* it is more like a shadow which obscures the original principle underlying it—its basis being no less than that spiritual principle of the *consciousness* of *Self*, which we shall consider later, and without which we can do nothing. As all the emphasis is usually placed upon the obvious unpleasantness and disadvantage of selfishness, it is well to remember that it is not an unmixed evil.

Selfishness may be defined as an undue attachment to one's own interest. I will pause to mention only a few of its many forms. Jealousy is a common one, being an attempt to claim that which is of no value unless freely given— it belongs to the intense and passionate natures as a rule, but cannot coexist with a large unselfish viewpoint.

Vanity and conceit are evidences of petty selfishness—extremely small views of the Self, with a consequent exaggeration of the personal self. Thoughtlessness of others arises from self-absorption and a limited horizon. All of these conditions can be overcome by a reasonable amount of practice and a true knowledge of the meaning of the *Self*—provided there is sufficient *desire* to make the effort; but people

who persist in marring their lives with these
and other outcroppings of the selfish spirit,
must be left to work out their own salvation—
no one can do it for them.

To pass from Selfishness to another more obviously negative state let us consider *Grief*.
All Pain is the evidence of the *absence* of something, and among our most acute pains is
that sense of loss called Grief. Although almost every one recognizes its destructiveness,
it nevertheless ranks among the most uncon-
trollable of the Emotions. There are few who
have yet learned the lesson of conscious adjustment, so that when affliction befalls them,
of whatever nature, they are able to accept it
calmly and without the shattering that seems
so unavoidable to those stricken with sorrow.
As a rule their behaviour displays the greatest
weakness, all centred around their own especial
deprivation. The mind refuses to work save in
the reiterated contemplation of its loss, and all
normal functions are reduced to their minimum.

While the utter lack of a capacity for Grief

would of course signify a lack of sensitiveness or power to feel bordering on the unhuman, there is almost always a desire to indulge in these devastating Emotions to the full. As we are always being beset by difficulties, it is one of those seemingly irresistible tendencies which it is most important to understand and control.

Even great personal losses as by death can be met with fortitude based upon a faith in the eternal goodness of all things. Such a view requires a detachment from a purely personal attitude, it is true, and a considerable amount of poise; but it brings its own reward. It is well to recognize in this connection that Grief in all its phases is based on a generic *instability,* is essentially selfish in its nature, and has no aspect of constructiveness in it.

Much Grief in the form of *regret* is wasted over various small losses, especially of purely material things. Perhaps it is small wonder that such is the case when it is a fact that most people gauge their happiness by the standard of whether they possess much or little. The dispossession of a trinket will sometimes occasion as much expenditure of feeling and force as would be required to construct an engine or write a book.

Those who have not yet risen above the bondage of mere things and of trivialities of all sorts are linked to a continual series of disappointments and regrets. The acquisition of things may be a pleasant pursuit and a means of producing happiness—popularity and good fortune are always to be desired—but when these become ends in themselves, the proportion is lost and some form of pain is inevitable—most of it unnecessary and wasted.

Closely allied to Grief is *Despondency,* or a mental depression of some duration and intensity. It is a common habit to those of much susceptibility, especially where the Imagination is well developed and the Will comparatively weak. In psychic impressionable natures it often takes the form of "apprehensiveness," a nameless fear or foreboding which cannot be readily thrown off. It has its origin in the subconscious life and is often most tenacious, even where the intentions are good. Being a

sticky, clammy state of mind, however, somewhat of the nature of a miasma, it cannot long
flourish in a wholesome and positive mentality.
It is really a pathological, emotional state due
to a sickness of the soul, but it can be cast
out like other dark-hued emotions with the cultivation of a healthy mental attitude.

"Moodiness" is another form of a disturbed
psychic life and is a dangerous indulgence when
carried to any extreme, calling for an active
control of the Will. All morbid mental states
throw a veil around the personality that tends
to smother its creator and depress its beholders.
Perhaps the worst of despondency is that it so
thoroughly envelops him who has once given
way to it, as to shut out all healthier, brighter
thoughts—all consciousness of light, truth, and
freedom. The only successful mode of treatment is preventive in character, establishing
opposite states of mind with such firmness that
the victim of his own feelings can no longer fall
into this abyss of misery.

The primary *Positive Emotions* are—

Confidence
Love
Joy
Expansiveness.

All of these represent the higher aspects of the consciousness—those furthest removed from the distinctly animal stage. *Confidence* might be considered an exception in its physical sense of self-preservation, but dealt with as a mental or emotional quality it contains within it the essence of all human achievement, and is, therefore, the most necessary among the traits to be strengthened or cultivated.

Self-confidence being closely allied to some of the lower and more disagreeable phases of the personality is often mistaken for them, being confused with mere egoism or conceit. The latter represent a fondness for the good opinion of others which is *not* characteristic of true self-confidence—a desire for approbation and attention being the direct outcome of a *lack* of egotism or right understanding of the dignity and power of the Self. An undue love of ap-

probation is a fundamental weakness tending
to undermine all the other virtues, none of
which can bloom without the nourishing influence of self-knowledge and self-belief. Any
mental structure reared without this primary
element lacks the strength and calibre to make
it stand.

It is amazing how in the training and development of children we manage to deprive
them of this one great force with which they
might attack life successfully. Ambition is
curbed and the desire to excel tapped at its
very root by the inculcation of self-distrust
and a consciousness of weakness or inability.
We seem to be afraid to give praise even when
praise is due.

Little do we realize the constructive force of
discriminating approval, even when the act
upon which it is bestowed is not all that we
could desire. The wise mother will, for example, commend her child for an attempt to
write or sew, even though the effort has been
most clumsy and the result poor. All things
are comparative in their value and when every

honest effort is rightly appreciated the results are proportionately great. Thus are laid the seeds of self-confidence which cannot be broken down by the hard knocks and disappointments of life.

So important is a real egotism that even that one who monopolizes attention, disregards the opinions of others and seems oversure of himself is much more to be admired and far happier than he who is beset by doubt and indecision and who is, therefore, inhibited in drawing upon his potential powers. While the distinction should always be kept clear between the pettiness, the thoughtlessness, and the unkindness that may arise from mere *egoism,* I cannot too much emphasize the need of a constant and vital *egotism,* as the one great antidote to fear and weakness.

Otherwise the feeling of self-depreciation insensibly gains the ascendancy simply by a mere force of habit. Each effort is disintegrated by carrying hidden within its core the seeds of destruction. I find, therefore, that in the majority of people constant affirmations are required to overcome this weakness and to develop the necessary "sense of self."

The self-confident mind and no other can give play to the natural instinct of *curiosity,* which is our only means of pushing ahead and acquiring the necessary knowledge of life. To lack in mental curiosity is to lack in initiative and therefore in experience. It is to remain "put," either paralyzed by fear or anaesthetized by sheer passivity. The curiosity of children should be encouraged, each question asked should be answered and true knowledge bestowed; for the curiosity that leads to the query is a positive manifestation and will become morbid and destructive only when turned in on itself, by reason of failure to secure the coveted information.

Curiosity in the sense of prying into other people's affairs is simply an *unbridled* and *unsympathetic* desire to "know." It lacks *discrimination* and develops mostly in cramped and narrow lives, or in the minds of those who have no true consciousness of Self and thus become aggressively occupied with the concerns of others.

To *feel* confident and sure is not only a much to be envied state but a most requisite one. If not blessed with it by nature, you should proceed to acquire it without further delay. It means *power* and so much does the world love power that it permits, or even encourages, an assumption of power by persons little fitted in point of character, but possessed of a certain aggressiveness of manner that impresses and overwhelms.

The common success of the charlatan or impostor, is a living proof of our admiration of real egotism even though we deny it. The fact that a persistent practitioner of fraud is really but preparing his own funeral does not deter us at all from bowing at the feet of the power he displays while he is successful.

All the more reason then why every effort should be made to inculcate a personal self-belief when one is working along lines of Truth; for a feeling of pride and confidence, of being able to create and achieve whatever our inner desires suggest to us, is indispensable to the sustenance of our vitality, happiness and success. Confidence is almost wholly a matter of the realization of the powers of the Self and it should come first in the development of the emotional life as it naturally does in the development of the race.

Next to confidence in point of importance and constructive force comes *Love*, that sympathetic and tender feeling which takes the individual out of his isolation and binds him to the rest of creation. All our ethical exhortations have for the past few centuries placed an emphasis upon Love, but we are in spite of this a long way from the comprehension, to say nothing of the application, of this supreme law of life.

It may be because we are now trying to develop affection and the social sense before having proceeded very far with the development of the individual and his *power* to love. It is like trying to draw a circle before knowing how to make a straight line; the former is but an extension of the latter and cannot be produced without a knowledge of line. The circle as a symbol represents the universal life, the straight line the individual life. Before we can experience the emotion of real Love, which is an outgoing from the Self to others, we must first experience *self-love,* or the recognition of Self. This is the manner of growth in the child and should have a significance for all students of Behaviour. I give thus briefly my reasons for placing Love second rather than first in the list of the Positive Emotions and I offer it also as a suggestion for a method to be developed for the education of the young.

Love in the abstract is the *attractive* principle in contradistinction to the aversion represented by Anger. Its tendency is all toward unity, fusion even, whereas the more primitive instinct leads to division and separateness. Fortunately for our happiness and the development of the race as a whole, Love is such a powerful instinct as to touch us all somewhere, sometime, even the animals showing many signs of this ennobling emotion.

But strong as it is, and salutary as it is, there is no one trait requiring more in the way of direction and control. Love is based on Desire, and when unrestrained it tends to covetousness and becomes the very antithesis of itself, swinging back from the unselfishness which is its core, into the supreme selfishness that shows as a wish for possession and ownership. This is the more common form as between men and women and usually characterizes most parental love as well.

Love, more than any other emotion, requires *Freedom* for its highest expression, and when we can understand the true meaning of the phrase "free love," not as an illegitimate passion between the sexes, but as a term descriptive of the real nature of man's most elevated feeling, we will be at the beginning of the great revelations which life has in store for us. I have already spoken of the Freedom of the Will, but the Freedom of Love is still greater. Carrying us as it does into the realms of the creative, super-physical, and spiritual life, we find in it the basis of all aspiration, religious feeling, and the instinct for humanitarianism which in different ways has characterized the race from its beginnings.

Love is naturally constructive, it develops thoughtfulness and protection for others, it enlarges the whole scope of the personality and is the only known antidote for selfishness. Not always however; for there is a tyranny of Love that is more destructive than its natural complement, hate. It threatens and coaxes, it drags and cajoles—and masters even while it abases.

We all need more Love, both to give and to receive it. We need the universal Love which makes us tolerant and kind. We need the personal Love which brings intimacy and understanding. And the great and unalterable law is, that we will *get* exactly as much of both of these as we are able and willing to *give*. Let us therefore cultivate one *power* to *love*, for it is the light of existence, and the only thing that will satisfy the soul's deepest craving.

Agreeability, in the sense of a good disposition, or kindly feeling, is an expression of Love

that perhaps has more to do with the comfort
and pleasantness of existence than any other
quality.   It is in itself merely a demeanour, but
is the evidence of a permanently sympathetic
attitude, which is the opposite of that disagree-
ableness of manner and uncordiality characteristic of those whose affective life harbours any
degree of resentment. Agreeability appears
in the individual when he is developed far
enough out of the habit of petty selfishness to
realize the feelings of others as he does of himself. It tends also to ease of manner and
adaptability; though when united with insincer-
ity, it becomes mere deceit and is of course no
longer constructive.

One of the most difficult problems for the self-
confident nature is to learn how to project itself into the lives and feelings of others. *Sympathy* is the means by which it is accomplished,
and any success in thus entering into unity with
another life is dependent upon the development
and combination of the love-feeling with a true
consciousness of one's own being. Curiously
enough, the emergence of one or the other of

these phases tends to obliterate its opposite, so that he who is full of sympathy and tenderness is seldom self-sufficient and virile; while he who gives evidence of these latter strong traits, is more apt to be inconsiderate, if not ruthless with others. But what an ideal is achieved when unto strength is added tenderness, as when love and sympathy are united with independent power.

By studying the feelings and probable desires of those about us we can learn to enter into their inner and psychic lives so as to become one with them, and relieve, by some sort of subtle telepathy their sense of aloneness. This is beyond doubt the very essence of the love-feeling and makes, automatically, the happiness of the loved one to become paramount.

Sympathy can very easily lose its positive character, however, and become merely maudlin or sentimental; or it may be the source of great weakness and trouble by taking one too far off one's own centre. Many times very antipathetic natures are bound by a kind of psychic sympathy or susceptibility that they cannot seem to escape. They forget that when Love ceases to be constructive it becomes an enemy calling aloud for vanquishment.

Appreciation is an important phase of Love that is too frequently overlooked. By Appreciation I do not mean gratitude—an emotion which like effusiveness, is dangerous because of its weakness—but a recognition of kindness and a desire to meet it in kind if possible. *Courtesy* is a conventionalized form of Appreciation and a most requisite one as a lubricant to the machinery of life.

Appreciation is a state of mind, which may not always be expressed in words but which can stand much more display than is ordinarily accorded it. This emotion, however, like many other phases of Feeling, especially those concerned with Love, is often neglected or even sternly repressed rather than encouraged and given vent. We seem to be ashamed of our finer feelings, and especially among men there is a common dread of giving evidence of any softness of heart. This is probably a remnant of our earlier and more savage life—in any case, it deprives us of one of the joys and constructive expressions of which we are so much in need.

Joy is the third in my list of Emotions calling for cultivation and care. Life presents so many difficulties to the average person as to lead him, by the time he has reached middle age at least, to doubt the reality of the existence of happiness and our habit is as a whole to look more upon the dark side of things than to dwell upon the brightness. By so doing much weight is added to our troubles, for we are missing the one salient fact in connection with the whole problem, which is that either joy or sadness exists *only in the mind* and is not a thing dependent upon the conditions of life.

To prove this we have only to look about us and see among many of those who are sorely pressed by want or sorrow, a spirit of true optimism and cheer. The valiant and happy are seldom among those whose circumstances would lead us to expect it of them.

As a matter of fact the gloom and mists of life are usually dissipated by a persistent spirit of cheer; certainly nothing adds so much to the ease with which tasks are accomplished and perplexities endured. We constantly vitalize our unhappy thoughts and conditions by *Attention*—things that would disappear of themselves quite readily are kept alive and active by the constant and depressing notice bestowed upon them.

Everything from physical pain to the deepest soul disappointment can be ameliorated by the application of a persistently joyful spirit. This is not a counsel to shallow optimism which refuses to see or admit the problems of life, but it is a very potent suggestion for the acquisition of that happiness which the whole world seeks. Joy is an affirmative attitude, and a state of mind dependent partly upon habit and partly upon an inward unity which gives one a feeling of well being which external conditions have not the power to disturb.

I think we should believe in happiness more than we do. Certainly nothing is more conducive to health, prosperity and achievement than to expect it and have faith in it. We

should not be afraid to be happy and to
give vent to it when we are, knowing that in so
doing we are spreading into some of life's dark
corners a true radiance. Happiness can be
cultivated by auto-suggestion until one rises to
that height of independence in his feelings that,
bring life what it may, he remains undisturbed
and possessed of his strongest and best weapon
—a joyful spirit. To have a capacity for joyful emotion, for enthusiasm, for unquenchable
spontaneity, like that of a child, supplies life
with the real zest and thrill it ought to
have.

To pass from Joy to the fourth in my list, I
have used the general term of *Expansiveness* to
represent the Emotion opposed to that of self-
love. My reasons for doing so will be apparent, I think, from the foregoing discussion of
the principal feelings that are grouped under
the heading of *positive*—they are all expansive
in character. Joy may be pictured as a straight
line going upwards, Expansiveness or Unselfishness can be indicated by a circle on a hori-
zontal plane—it suggests breadth and inclu-

siveness, it does away with the contractions that are always consequent upon the feelings of Fear, Grief, and Anger.

On the mental plane Expansiveness means breadth and catholicity of thought, freedom from prejudice and provincialism. On the emotional plane it means sociability, frankness, liberality, and affection. It is geniality and openness of spirit as opposed to secretiveness, shyness, envy, rivalry, acquisitiveness, coldness and snobbishness. *Eleutherian* is a Greek word meaning "like a free man, freely giving, bountiful," and it seems to me the best to describe the antithesis of the narrowness of self-love. Truly it is the mark of the enlightened soul.

Really, Expansiveness means to dive into life up to the hilt, which is what the selfish person never does. It is the only means of obtaining real knowledge, there is little gained in standing to one side and watching life pass by. He who has a zest for experience with an equal willingness to be enough of a "sport" to pay the necessary price in pain for his knowledge, is the one who, if he survives, is the strongest and best fitted to be a leader among his fellow men. But the inhibitory feelings often master; one of the strongest of them is the dread of making mistakes, than which there can be no greater restraint from the fulness of life. Even the worst of crimes is not life at its weakest and poorest, it is rather life at its fullest and best, turned, perhaps by a trifling incident, in the wrong direction.

Why stop so much to question whether the impulse be right or wrong? To dillydally over one's feelings and convictions, to weigh and compare them with others, to analyze, is but to lose the capacity for emotion and the power to act. It is far better to do *something* than to do nothing through doubt or indecision. Whether one be resolutely virtuous or the most hardened sinner is of less import than whether one has the freedom of Will and the courage of his conviction to *live* as he sees fit. The prevalence of the critical and prejudiced spirit, the great ignorance of one-half of the world as to how the other half lives, are but evidences of the *pau-*

city of our Emotions as a whole and our dread
of increasing the meagre store.

To have experienced something usually means
to have understood it, at least in some degree;
and nothing is a better cure for narrowness and
selfishness than actual contact with the breadth,
depth, and power of human Emotions. With
experience one may pass from the kindergarten
to the university in the realm of Feelings quite
as much ·as in the life of the Intellect. One
learns in time to discard the impulses which
are useless and curb those which are dangerous
—one gains the courage to *dare to feel,* as well
as to guard against satiety.

The Emotions are ofttimes treated, it is true,
with the same disregard that the drunkard
treats his body, with a resulting loss of sensitiveness and freshness and power. The modern man's "brainstorm" or the hysterical
woman's uncontrolled outbursts are but emotional orgies showing an excitability and excess
that can only react to their serious detriment.
Nothing runs away with us so quickly as Feelings, and especially those that are indulged in

for their own sake. The woman who "enjoys
poor health," or the man who "carries a chip
on his shoulder," the habitually "injured" person, the sexual pervert, the religious fanatic,
are all from the same stem and are in sad need
of regulation and self-government. But these
are excrescences on life's tree and have no
bearing on the essential soundness of our innate Feelings and our privilege of luxuriating
in them.

Broadly speaking, Emotions may be divided,
and usually are, into the two general groups of
Pleasure and *Pain*. There has always been
contention between the various schools of
metaphysics as to which of these was the positive and which the negative state, some claiming that Pain was due merely to the absence
of Pleasure and was, therefore, the positive
one; while others, claiming that Pleasure was
due to cessation of Pain, stated *it* as the positive one. Without attempting here to solve the
old question of whether evil "exists" or not,
I wish to make it plain that as a working philosophy of life, I have found nothing to equal

that which chooses *Pleasure* as its positive element and believes therefore that *Pain* is negative. This gives Pain the same kind of reality the darkness possesses, which is not much, as we know by seeing how easily it can be dissipated with the appearance of the light.

Perhaps Pleasure and Pain will always exist in about equal parts, somewhat the same as the phenomena of day and night. I daresay Pain is quite as necessary a reaction to life as Pleasure is; but in our present state of development it is possible to place the *emphasis* upon the pleasurable Emotions—certainly Pain should never be sought for its own sake as it sometimes is, especially by the habitual melancholic, or the emotional fanatic who thus finds an outlet for feelings he does not understand how to otherwise express.

Where unavoidable Pain must be stoically endured; but if our habit were only to search more deeply for causes, and we could recognize Pain, as we should, as a sign that we were on the wrong track, it would not be long before we could eliminate most of our painful experiences.

Pain whether physical or mental is a danger
signal to warn us that we are out of order somewhere, and that it is "up to us" to find the
cause and set it right. Instead of this, all our
attention is given to Pain as a symptom—the
Pain-consciousness is positively acute in most
people—and their readiness to experience, en-
large upon, and apparently revel in sensations
of discomfort of all kinds, be they mental or
physical, is but a commentary upon the present
perversity of human nature. No allowance is
made for natural adaptability, for powers of
endurance, or for the Reason with which we are
endowed, by means of which the distress might
be ameliorated or excised.

There is a chronic form of Pain called *hy-
peraesthesia*—it is a sort of moral and emotional sensitiveness which makes almost everything in one's environment to become painful,
producing a state of high tension and excitability difficult of comprehension by the less
complex and more stolid nature. It might
fairly be rated a pathological condition; and
while it calls for some tenderness in handling,

the only real relief for these sufferers is to get
a better balance by the development of greater
ruggedness in their emotional-physical natures.

It has been said that one's power of enjoyment is measured by one's capacity for Pain
—a truth worth pondering, since it shows how
perfectly balanced are all laws and all elements
in one's life, and how one must reach in both
directions in order to extend the ability to Feel.
It is true that if one is capable of deep suffering, one is also capable of a greater appreciation of the things that go to make for satisfaction and joy, and one should not be afraid of
either direction.

I shall not attempt to write a homily on the
"uses of adversity," since I believe much more
in the uses of good fortune; but we cannot
afford to overlook the undoubted fact that Pain
is superior in its *volitional efficacy;* for it does
drive us to action, and increases the life-scope
as nothing else can. The reason is, that all
Pain being due to an absence of some of the
vital powers of life or to their harmonious

workings, forces us because of its discomfort to remedy the defect.

Hence, in a way, troubles are good for us. We have only to look to the infant to see how completely his reactions to life are established by his various pain-experiences—he seeks food because he suffers pain without it, and he avoids the things that hurt because after a certain number of repetitions he cannot but associate them with the pain-sensation. I do not offer this fundamental truth in the belief that it will afford any great comfort to my suffering reader, but only to help him to a little philosophy as to the reason for the existence of Pain and to show him that in himself lies the key to an ultimate escape from it.

Both Pleasure and Pain emerge from a neutral state which is prior to and distinct from both of them. This state might be called *Contentment* and in its immature phases represents an embryonic stage like that of the seed which has not yet developed its potential powers. In our progress through Life and Emotion we swing from one extreme to the other, from

Pleasure to Pain and back again until we finally gain a fine equilibrium, a state of superiority to either one, which might again be called Contentment or *imperturbability*. It is not, however, the Contentment of ignorance, stagnation or lack of feeling, it is rather the measure that accrues to one who has glimpsed the whole arc of human experience. This was what the Stoics of old worked for and it is not beyond the attainment of the modern student of Psychology who knows that it is his own attitude toward life that determines whether Pain or Pleasure shall predominate with him.

Although Control and Stoicism are among the most admirable virtues, my reader will have gathered by now that the positive Emotions should all represent in some way the natural law of *Expression*, the unfolding and showing forth of the instinctive life forces. The great crime of civilization has been its ruthless suppression of all the natural feelings. All the way through it has struggled to overlay the purely human elements with the restraining and artificial domination of the Intellect, until today, in all social intercourse at least, the emotional life is seriously maimed and almost useless. This implies a grave loss of force and spontaneity; and in addition there are various emotional complications resulting from the holding back and retention of feelings which in the natural course of things should be expressed.

Ideas which in themselves may be quite harmless ferment and produce destructive reactions when checked and held in suspension in the subconsciousness. For as we have already seen, to "forget" a thing is not to destroy it. Mere intellectual concepts may quickly fade away into nothingness, but *Feelings,* once generated, do not dissipate themselves without having left their mark and produced reactions that may continue indefinitely according to the amount of force that was created or expended. This important psychological fact and the unceasing antagonism between the critical objective consciousness and the uncritical but powerful urge of vitality in the subconsciousness accounts for the constant "surge" of the emotional life and explains most of the inconsistencies of human behaviour.

The greatest conflict is between the primordial craving of the soul for life, love, and activity and the many restrictions imposed by social conditions upon the expression of that craving. The resulting disquietude is a characteristic element in the subconsciousness of practically every one and is thus a social problem as well as an individual one. Fortunately it can be solved individually, so that happiness and harmony will be manifested on the external plane in the natural course. There is quite a distinction between working to settle this antagonism in one's self, and making an antagonist of society by blaming it for all one's ills. It is not so necessary to break with established customs in order to satisfy those cravings which seem to go counter to the conventions, as it is to secure a harmonious internal adjustment.

To completely harmonize the conscious and unconscious life requires much knowledge and intellectual endowment and it is a problem upon which we are just embarking in any conscious scientific way. It might be said to be *the* problem of human life today.

I find it comparatively simple to secure the desired results in responsive individuals, though it is more difficult to formulate laws and methods that are applicable to all cases. The all-important fact to be taken into consideration is that Thoughts and Feelings once repressed on account of their painful nature, or never recognized, do continue to be active and operate along lines of their own in the subconsciousness. We know that they repeatedly attempt to arise to consciousness and that because of our wish to forget or our refusal to recognize them there, they are forced to assume various disguises and emerge in unexpected or substitute forms. Thus is often revealed to us a thought or wish that we never believed we could have entertained, thus do we experience various "mental landslides" when unknown or long latent parts of the subconsciousness suddenly rise to the surface causing dire confusion.

The skilled Psychologist through long experience is able to recognize many of these disguised expressions at once and knows his ":types" as thoroughly as does the biologist. The fundamental theory of Psycho-analysis is that the symptoms of hysterical patients (of which there is a much wider class than is generally supposed) depend upon impressive but forgotten scenes in their lives. The treatment consists in causing the patients to recall and reproduce these experiences in consciousness, a process very properly designated as *catharsis,* because the whole idea is to *eliminate* the *source* of the trouble. The symptoms themselves represent undischarged centres of excitement and only require conversion into normal channels for relief to ensue—hence the necessity of the "clearing-out" process.

To give a simple but common example, it is a habit in a certain type of woman to try and conceal a recognized sex-attraction. She does this by feigning a coldness she does not feel. The wish to repress any evidence of her feelings turns the natural eagerness and desire into an appearance of repulsion, producing a cold and disagreeable manner. The real feeling is of course the exact opposite of this and if of any intensity leads either to hysteria or to recklessness.

The cure obviously is to effect a compromise between the desire to show feeling and the equally strong one to hide it. Unless the case is a chronic or unusually severe one, a *recognition* of the internal conflict followed by a reasonable amount of expression such as the conventions permit, will equalize the pressure sufficiently to allow the psychic life to become normal. The display of aversion is clearly the result of too much fear in the first place and an inability to be natural. This fear takes refuge in the common convention that a woman must not show her feelings in relation to the opposite sex, and produces an unconscious *impasse* resulting in a more or less serious mental and physical disturbance.

The method here outlined sounds simple enough, but is, as a matter of fact, a most difficult and delicate process even where the sub-

ject of the operation accords her conscious co-
operation. It must be remembered that the
very presence of her trouble is an indication
of a subconscious rebellion. Sometimes many
weeks, or even months, are required to effect
the needed change; but the mere fact that it
can be done at all is one of the marvels of modern psychological achievement.

There are many other situations dissimilar
to this one, which call for the same principle
in treatment. Mental jars and emotional crises
seldom pass without leaving a scar of some
kind, so that the old wounds need to be re-
opened and thoroughly cleansed before health
and comfort can be properly restored.

Most conflicts of this nature could be avoided
if we were more willing to realize our nearness
to the life of the primitive plane from which
as a race we are not very far removed in spite
of all our development. Furthermore, the
moral distinctions that have come with the
gradual unfolding of man's higher nature are as
yet almost entirely arbitrary and superficial,
giving rise to endless conflicts, doubts, and in-

compatibilities. Thus the internal moral-emotional life becomes a hot-bed of dissension. We usually try to settle it by accepting the conventional dictums, at the same time denying them vigorously in our secret thoughts and feelings.

Many there are, for instance, who subscribe to the established religious customs of the day purely because it gives them a comfortable feeling to think that somebody or something is upholding our "morals." As for actually putting into practice the precepts they pretend to admire, they will tell you, if frank, that it is quite impossible, that the ideals are impracticable and beyond the reach of human nature!

Such as these never stop to question the futility of an ideal that is not *believed* in, much less do they realize the danger accruing from the psychological anomaly thus created. Sometimes they succeed in adapting themselves to this curious double standard and so escape to some extent the suffering consequent upon trying to go two ways at one time. The more sincere the person, the greater his problem, although real sincerity is usually backed up by a strength enabling him to solve the question definitely one way or another. He does not then subscribe to one code of action while his heart and belief are in another, or delude himself by shallow hypocrisy.

This whole question merely indicates that the emotional life has up to the present time been *unregulated,* left to the mercy of fancy, whim, or headlong impulse. The only regulation we have known has been that built upon stern precepts concerned with unpleasant words like "duty," "punishment," or "being found out." A control imposed only by outward necessity is no control at all—an unwilling obedience is valueless because it does not touch the heart. I shall not further moralize. What is paramount is an *agreement* in one's self, a balancing and blending of all the Emotions and a willingness to accept into consciousness *all* our impulses however contrary or ignoble they may seem.

Herein lies the crux of the whole matter. It is not necessary to give expression in the form of *action* to those Emotions which we know

are destructive, or "wrong" as we like to call
it. There must always be the curb of the Will
and the supremacy of the higher nature, but
there are means of escape from this seemingly
irreconcilable situation, whereby we can maintain the proper restraint and yet at the same
time find expression or reconciliation for the
impulses that are usually inhibited.

The first of these consists, as we have already
seen, in the simple recognition by the conscious
mind of the inhibition. Most of our primitive
impulses are so far buried that we are no longer
aware of their existence and a certain amount
of analytical probing is most salutary, in turning up to consciousness elemental forces that
we have consciously or unconsciously repressed.

This is the Freudian method and an important one, even though they place too much emphasis upon the analytical process with a corresponding weakness on the constructive side.
For while the raising into consciousness of some
forgotten or inhibited emotional complex is
often sufficient to eliminate the disturbance and
restore harmony, it is in a comparatively small

proportion of cases that this happy result accrues without a subsequent careful *synthesis* of all the elements that have been torn apart in the effort to extract the offending member.

To perform this operation as it is done by the average present-day Psycho-analyst is like having a surgical process for the removal of a tumour without any succeeding medical care for the upbuilding of the weakened constitution. The mind is a delicate instrument and the application to it of the analytical process is more than likely to produce a mental shock of some kind, a reaction simple or violent according to the extent of the original damage. The Christian Scientists call it a "chemicalization" and all Mental Scientists know the symptoms even though unacquainted, as often happens, with the rationale of their treatment.

The disturbing reaction, while practically unavoidable in the nature of the circumstances, need not last long however, when a wise manipulator is in charge of the case. The subject of right psychological treatment quickly regains his poise and finds himself upon a much higher plane than before the operation; but the treatment is only just begun. The subject—or the patient, as it usually happens, since Repression always makes one ill ultimately—must first learn something of his own mental processes and be led step by step into a reorganization of them on a more harmonious and stronger basis.

The real means of escape from the conflict between Nature and Intellect lies in the process called *Transmutation,* in which we can consciously recognize and raise to a higher form of expression feelings that in their primitive state would not be constructive or fitting to our environment.

Thus the common craving for *Love,* if restrained might lead to a destructive anti-social conduct. The craving for Love is however a natural and legitimate feeling and should be so recognized. If it cannot be satisfied in the ordinary course of circumstances, it can be transmuted or changed on to some other plane of expression. In the case of the unmarried woman for example, whose instinctive wants are apt to be blighted, it is possible for her to find relief and satisfaction in certain constructive occupations where there is an outlet for her creativeness and desire to *give*.   Better still, and even necessary in some instances, if her repressed emotions can find expression in some kind of an affectionate attachment—perhaps for a child, where the maternal instinct comes into play and the responsiveness evoked from the child is such as to supply the needed heart-interest. A different form of Transmutation is that achieved by the artist, who through his creative imagination turns his various haunting ideas and generative impulses into works of art rather than into actions, thus obtaining both production and relief.

The Psycho-therapist is confronted with a great variety of problems, all calling for endless ingenuity in developing a constructive adaptability in the many *déséquilibrés* who come to him for treatment.   The larger his experience in life, the wider the range of his sympathies and the greater his aspirational qualities, the more successful will he be in helping them to acquire the needed strength and balance.

Of these psychological difficulties there are many varieties with symptoms ranging all the way from simple "nervousness" through the *neuroses* and *psychoses,* to complete insanity. The great affliction of mental unbalance may be said to be almost wholly due to emotional repression of some sort, throwing too much weight upon a single idea or feeling. The pity is that life is so adamantine in some of its demands that the good of the individual is so often overlooked and sacrificed. Psychotherapy is filling a great need and doing a great work in this field where untold suffering has so long been without remedy.

So many emotional states are purely "substitute" ones in the effort of the conscious self to avoid a painful issue. Various "gusts" of feeling are thus likely to rise unbidden, possibly in the form of unreasonable anger, or as unexpected "tendernesses," or in excessive or misplaced mirth. What is called a "nervous laugh" is always the evidence of obstruction to some desire, usually one concerned with the affectional nature.

The whole subject of laughter is of the utmost importance in this connection, but as several notable treatises have been devoted to this topic especially, I will not say more here than to recommend normal wholesome laughter as one of the best possible outlets for accumulated feelings. The popularity of light amusement and entertainments that tickle the sense of humour all have a perfectly sound psychological basis. In practically all forms of wit and humour as well as many other modes of naïve expression, the heart of man instinctively lays bare its hidden motives. In excess all these expressions become hysterias, phobias, or some kind of mental compulsion beyond control of the conscious Will.

But a readiness to see the "funny" side of things, a real sense of humour, is indeed the saving grace of life and does more than anything else to preserve the mental balance. He who can secure sufficient detachment to be amused at himself is in little danger of carrying bruised feelings about with him or becoming the victim of a "sore spot" or abrasion in his own mind. Wit finds expression in intellectual form but is essentially an emotional experience—one to be sedulously fostered and indulged in, without *too* much respect to circumstance or fitness. It is a particularly effectual means of Transmutation, though it might be better if the subject were more often aware of what repression he is giving vent to in his spontaneous moods.

This leads me to a consideration of the second means of reconciling the opposition always present between the primitive Emotions and the Intellect. It is a matter of *Education,* though not in the usual fashion, for it consists in encouraging and developing the sensuous or emotional side of life—learning how to abandon oneself to all forms of Feeling that are not intrinsically destructive. Herbert Spencer said, "Whatever moral benefit can be effected by education must be effected by an education which is *emotional* rather than *perceptive.*"

And what is Emotional education? It is learning to utilize that which is conceived in the Imagination and developed through the

Senses; it is spontaneity, creativeness, a sense of comradeship and friendly competition, and, above all, the power of passing without break from thought and fancy into act. It includes as a matter of course a recognition of obstacles and limitations, but only as challenges to a fuller expression of a power that is felt to be inherent.

One of the earliest and most instinctive forms of Sense-education is *imitation* and *make-believe*. Every child lives in a world of his own creation which is for the most part a reproduction in miniature of the life he sees enacted about him. It is closely allied to the *play-instinct,* which is an intrinsic delight in activity for its own sake without any ulterior motive such as the Intellect always supplies in later life.

Play is an expression of sensuous freedom, it supplies refreshment by means of the *release* it allows the simple unaffected spontaneity native to childhood—it bubbles forth without the consideration and calculation that is essential in maturer years when *work* becomes the order of the day.

Work is imposed, necessitous, restraining—
though the wise man is careful to choose a
work that is *play* to him. If successful in this,
his occupation does not drain and fatigue him,
but serves more or less as recreation does, to
release his inner desires which are the natural
incentive to all activity. Any restraint can be
borne, however, if it is relieved with frequent
intervals of play. We speak of the "play"
of the imagination, of "playing" the piano,
phrases indicative of some of the means at
our disposal for emotional expression. It is
change, not rest, that we need; and especially
a faculty for *luxuriating in the realm of the
purely sensuous.*

It is a matter for serious consideration in
this over-intellectualized age, to develop by definite intention the simple functions of the five
senses—sight, hearing, smell, taste, and touch
—things almost forgotten in their finer manifestations except by the epicure or aesthete.
Sensuous perception is dulled in most of us.
We do not see colours, hear delicate sounds,
smell or taste with any sensitiveness; and as

for touch, who but the blind or those deprived of some one of the normal senses is able to draw upon anything like the fulness of this marvellous means of perception. The power to gain pleasure from stroking an old Greek vase, or to stoop and caress the violets as Tennyson was known to do, is a sign of strength as well as exquisite sensuousness.

There is no better avenue for the projection of the sensuous, impulsive creative self than in a true appreciation of and participation in the various art-forms. As a race we are sadly in need of the development of the natural aesthetic instinct. Of course, Intellect enters to some extent into all aesthetic attitudes; but Emotion is the stronger element and makes for a sort of detached interest, contemplative in its nature and without desire for consideration of practical utility.

To be able to thus enjoy things that have no utilitarian value is a sign not only of a developed mind, but of developed Emotions as well, and is one of the higher pleasures dependent upon civilization and culture. It must be remembered, however, that culture is not a matter of books or acquired formulas, it is simply being "human" and it comes from a wide and sympathetic contact with people. It grows out of the *play-spirit* far more than it does out of the university or the cloister. We all love the *natural* person, thus paying a compliment, even though unwittingly, to the emotional power and lack of self-consciousness that combine to produce real spontaneity.

To tell the truth, we love all Feeling but are too civilized and artificial to admit it. We show how much we love it by going to the theatre where we can enjoy it by proxy or in secret as it were—where the villain can be as villainous and the heroine as beautiful and sentimental as one could wish. We thus momentarily create the illusion that *we* are experiencing these things. The greatest applause is bestowed by the audience when the players give expression to some sentiment of which they approve and not when the *art* of presenting these emotions is at its best or highest. This is quite as it should be, since the latter requires an *aesthetic* appreciation and is therefore largely intellectual, while the sentiment expressed allows a real opportunity for self-dramatization —a very vital human matter as we have already seen.

The actors and their parts do indeed symbolize the various phases of our own personalities and in their tragic conflicts represent to us our own emotional battles. The very human desire that all shall come out happily in the end of the play expresses the inherent wish in every heart for harmony and fitness in life.

Our need of dramatic representations is all the more acute because we do not ordinarily dare to confess our own feelings and the extent to which we are subject to the very things we deny. The stage supplies this deficiency to a considerable extent and also enlarges the scope of our emotional life because it develops situations which we as individuals would never be likely to experience. We would therefore be far more normal and happy if the universal dramatic instinct which shows itself so naturally in childhood were to be truly cherished

and developed. The results would be still
more efficacious if we were ourselves the actors
instead of being only detached spectators.

The present-day movement for the commu-
nity-drama is a move in the right direction and
will do much for life in America if it can ever
be popularized to the point of becoming spontaneous and natural to any large number of
people. We love little children because they
exhibit and take pleasure in that instinctive
part of their being which we as adults have
grown to dislike and fear. But before we can
give expression to our natural feelings with
all the directness, simplicity, and power native
to children, *and without apology,* we shall have
to grow much.

Next to the Drama, *Music* is the most universally available of all our art-expressions. It
has the added advantage of being the most subjective and therefore the simplest and most
sensuous. To understand and get the most out
of modern music requires of course a certain
amount of knowledge and training, but this re-
fers to the technique of its production and has

little to do with the relaxation and sensuous enjoyment to be obtained from almost any kind of harmonious sound. Music should not be approached intellectually—the essential thing is to *listen* and to *feel*—let the thinking come afterward.

The invention of the modern piano is a practical help in the development of the emotional life, as it has made music available in the homes of nearly every one. This has been increased by the still later development of music produced mechanically, thus doing away with the necessity for the acquisition of a personal technique—though the disadvantages are obvious.

Every one who is the owner of a musical instrument should encourage the habit of musical improvisation. Merely letting the hands wander over the keys without much consideration of form or rhythm serves both as recreation and self-expression. Every one should sing also—both alone and in choruses. Even mechanical music has, generally speaking, a soothing effect and can be utilized in a practical way

by reproducing records of the impulses and
emotional concepts that appeal to us the most.
We thus have an opportunity of entering into
the internal experiences of great geniuses and
extending our own perceptions accordingly.

Closely allied to Music is *Dancing*, than which
there is no finer art-expression. It is primordial and instinctive like Music and has the
added value of uniting bodily activity with the
psychic and emotional appreciations aroused
by the other arts. A certain amount of dancing or its equivalent is really essential to any
well balanced life; not so much the conventionalized forms prevalent in the modern ballroom
—though they have their uses—but the more
aesthetic forms which give vent to a refined
play-instinct and the creative imagination.
The pantomime-dance especially is valuable.
As a picturing out of the various emotions it is
symbolical, full of significance, expresses many
delicate nuances of feeling; that is to say it has
the essential and fundamental character of aesthetic creation, proceeding entirely from material within the dancer's consciousness.

The plasticity and beauty as well as the sensuousness of dancing is almost universally admired, but like so many of our emotional pleasures we prefer to pay others to do it for us— we would rather sit and watch a dancer than to be human enough or natural enough to take part in the demonstration ourselves. Dancing, especially improvisation, should be as much a part of our emotional education as instrumental music—if we would all start the day by a little private séance in which we danced and acted out our inmost feelings, not only the day would be richer, but the whole of life.

Painting and *Drawing* are arts which owing to the need of a technique are less available to everybody than the art-forms just mentioned. They are nevertheless of exceeding importance in the development of the emotional life and of much wider applicability than is generally believed. Since Drawing and Painting have been introduced into our public school systems, there has been full and amazing evidence of the universality of this power of representation— even what we call talent is so frequent as to be

most surprising to those who have given the
subject little thought.

There is, however, every reason why this
faculty should be present in all of us, as it is
the most natural instinct imaginable to wish
to re-present our thoughts by means of drawn
symbols. It is in most cases merely latent—
due again to the restraints of civilization and
intellectual forms of education. Primitive man
instinctively produced symbols and images
which today we prize as true artistic treasures,
little realizing that we could all do about as
well if not better, were we allowed some freedom in the matter from infancy on.

Craftsmanship is that combination of a love
of beauty with utilitarianism which has in recent years again become more popular as a
means of personal expression than has been the
case since the wide introduction of machinery.
The efficiency and economy of machine made
articles has threatened to entirely stifle the expression of that beautiful and fitting human desire to make with our own hands the things
needed for household and personal use and

adornment. We owe much to William Morris and his collaborators for re-inspiring the spirit of personal craftsmanship, and if we are wise we will teach not only our children but ourselves the value and superiority of handmade things. We will not neglect this wholesome and useful form of aesthetic self-expression.

This projection of the self, especially of the Emotional self, into objective and permanent forms is highly valuable as a means of materializing the life of the Imagination. It is essentially an expression of Feeling, and all art that departs from this primary law departs also from its essential function and therefore its greatest value. The modern movement in the art world is "Impressionistic" in type —that is, it aims to produce certain emotions in its beholders rather than exact representations of material objects. Even though some of its efforts to thus divorce Intellect from Emotion have been grotesque in the extreme, the tendency itself is not only valuable from an artistic point of view, but is of great import as a promise of a freer and more sensuous expression in all life.

The love of *Beauty* is in itself probably the highest form of aspiration of which the human soul is capable. It is Love in its most impersonal and therefore its most spiritual form; it is passion sublimated to the nth degree; it is also an emotional outlet, and he who has not yet learned the joy of an appreciation of Beauty in some form is indeed barren and drear. We need in America especially to cultivate this sense—in Literature, in Civics, in Architecture, in Decoration, and in our personal lives.

In Europe it is much more a part of the life of the people, owing to their age-long art traditions. The Beauty-lover finds in the Old World much more to satisfy and feed him, much more of the "atmosphere" in which he likes to bask. We have to thank the Latin peoples not only for their art-forms but for the fine Emotions and passionate impulses which gave birth to the art-life that is so characteristic of them.

If we could but tear away our sedateness, our proprieties, and our worship of Ideas rather than of Feelings, we would be free of the greatest hampering elements in our self-elected paths of progress. Freedom means neither license nor immorality, though unfortunately it is associated with these ideas in the minds of most. Real freedom, as we have already observed, has its first essential in *self-expression* and is therefore the very basis of a constructive emotional life.

But while pleading for *expression,* I shall pause long enough to draw attention to one more phase of it—an unbridled and excessive one which is all too common. I speak of *Intoxication,* a state in which there is generally a real riot of Emotion. It is usually induced artificially by means of drugs or liquor, though there are many kinds of "drunks" besides this one. In the chapter on Imagination we have already seen how the creative side of the mentality finds more freedom when the usual inhibitions of objective Intellect are thus removed.

It is this desire subconsciously apprehended which leads to drink as a vent for repressed Emotions. It is a common sight to see any one who is under the influence of liquor behaving exactly opposite to his usual habit. The man who is well behaved and considerate in his normal state will become quarrelsome and even violent when the censorship of Intellect and Will is weakened or removed. Likewise it is a common phenomenon to see unusual affection or sentimentality displayed when the discriminating appraisal of pride and mastery is absent. These are but signs of impulses from which the embargo has been removed, and should make us pause long enough to better understand the nature of the intense longing that is the downfall of so many.

Drinking to excess is a *symptom,*—it shows a marked loss of psychic balance, and may, in irregulated lives, be a useful and even a necessary escape valve. It is for this reason a serious matter to inflict compulsory prohibition. It is not really legitimate to shut off the only means of emotional release available to the majority, until a constructive substitute is provided.

To do so is merely to strike at symptoms, not causes. There is no value, either practical or moral, in preventing the *act* while the cause remains untouched—I with Mark Twain, "hate those enemies of the human race who go around enslaving God's free people with *pledges*—to quit drinking instead of to quit *wanting* to drink"!

To really alter the desire-life enough to purge the world of this, one of its greatest evils, would mean subconscious re-education on a wholesale plan and is not at the present time practical except in individual cases. Therefore nothing but damaging explosions can be expected with the shock-absorber of intoxication entirely removed. If all lives were worked out on a normal basis there would be no need of, and practically no desire for, spirituous liquors. Even as a stimulant they would be unnecessary, because in a sane and balanced life, the natural Emotions would supply sufficient motive power without external aids. It is only where one is fighting against one's self that drugs are needed to dull the sensibilities. The man who "drinks to drown his sorrow" is merely following the line of least resistance, dreading to meet the issue squarely of his loss. If he but knew it, he only defers that day when he must really solve his problem with an active Will and manly courage.

It is plain to be seen that advantageous and attractive as the expression of Emotion is, it must be tempered and united with a controlling Intellect. Yet there are many times—and these are the things that I feel most impelled to impress upon my readers—when Intellect should be utterly abandoned and deserted.

One *must,* in order to be truly responsive, whether it be in the purely human relations or in an appreciation of the abstract virtues such as Wisdom, Truth, and Beauty, be able to be like a harp upon which the winds of life are playing—able to give forth in the many and varied forms that life affords, an expression of true sensibility, a responsiveness that knows no bounds.

I have tried within the brief span of a chapter to give some survey of the Emotions as a whole, though all that can be said is cold and inadequate as compared to the dominant part played

by the passions in human life. If I have succeeded in pointing the way toward the balance
that is possible between seemingly irresistible
emotional tendencies and the arrestive power of
the Will, my efforts will not be without value.

It is probable that in the perusal of my observations on the subject each of my readers will
find that certain profound and more or less
hidden states of feeling have arisen to his consciousness. This also is a practical result
which if achieved cannot fail to be of considerable personal value. While the foregoing study of the Emotions is far from being
exhaustive, it should serve as a sort of diagram-
matic starting point for the sincere student
who finds the study of human impulses not only
of great fascination, but of the greatest service in pointing the way to that superior life
which we all, in our hearts, believe and hope
for.

The following study on "Sex" is an effort to
supply in part, the characteristic omission or
deficiency in the treatment of this most vital
of all the Emotions.

CHAPTER VI

SEX

THE PSYCHOLOGY OF THE CREATIVE LIFE

SEX, as every one knows, is, with the exception of *self-preservation,* the strongest and most vital of the human instincts. Its importance to the individual and to the race as a whole is manifestly paramount, and the day has come when we must fling aside our conventional attitudes and dare to search into its meaning and manifestations, with at least the same sincerity we approach other and less vital subjects. I have devoted a chapter to Sex in this volume, not only because it is a subject encrusted with the most dense and dangerous ignorance, but because it has more to do with the shaping of our Behaviour and our destiny than any other single force or influence in life.

Let the reader who would decry or doubt this

statement be very frank and honest with himself (or herself as the case may be, as women are less likely to admit it than men) and if such a one does not agree with me after a careful reading it will be for one or two reasons; either through ignorance of the facts of life, or, through prejudice and bad training, he is too disturbed by the truth to want to admit it into his consciousness.

At first glance it seems inexplicable to the unbiased student of life, that anything so centrally concerned with our very existence, and so evidently capable of causing both the greatest happiness and the greatest harm, should have been so sedulously kept in its chambers of darkness, breeding endless errors and destruction, when it should have been above all other things a matter of earnest study and a light on the path as to the significance of life.

The reason is not far to seek however. The vast range of sexual activities and their undisputed dominion over the destinies of men, even though but dimly apprehended, has overwhelmed us with a sense of futility and caused us to ignore and shrink from its power—like ostriches in the sand. It is *fear* that has kept us from a knowledge of the Great Mystery; and woe unto him who dares to disturb the world's sleep by tearing away any of the veils before the Temple! Yet some one must speak the word to dispel the darkness that beclouds the Truth and even a small contribution to our limited and distorted knowledge is indispensable from the point of view of the progress and welfare of both the individual and the race.

What then *is* Sex? That no real definition exists is but one of the many stumbling blocks in the way of our path to knowledge. Certainly Sex is not a mere anatomical distinction with its implications of physical attraction; and neither is it *a state of mind,* although it gives rise to innumerable psychological manifestations of the most profound sort. It must be seen clearly, at the outset, that Sex is a discarnate thing, an *abstraction,* and quite beyond the reach, in its entirety, of the mind of man. We can, however, dimly recognize it as a *Principle*—a universal creative Force, im-

manent and profound, an Energy, showing itself forth in humanity as an Instinct and an
Emotion truly titanic in its proportions.

I have chosen in this study to regard Sex as
the great Emotion, albeit somewhat abstractly.
To treat of it at all adequately I must depart
from the more closely psychological method
which I have followed up to this point, for the
pertinent reason that there is as yet no established Psychology of Sex; also any study of
the motives activating the sex-life, must, to
be of value, include a *philosophy* of Sex, a
consideration of its origin, nature and purpose,
which is much wider than is generally supposed.

Such research as has been made has been
almost entirely physiological in character, treat-
ing Sex as a physical instinct only, with the
single purpose of propagation as its end and
raison d'être. *Love* has, of course, been dealt
with in relation to Sex, but only as implying
the *addition* of a certain degree of tenderness
to simple sexuality—while some, regarding
Love as a higher evolution and self-existent,
have differentiated it entirely from the sex-in-

stinct. But elevating Love to the dignity of
an Emotion (which as we will remember is
merely a conscious awareness of an instinct)
does not divorce or separate it in any way
from its sexual origin and foundation.

Sex, like many other Forces and Feelings,
becomes very complex when it rises from the
animal into its human manifestations, and takes
on a different cast, as it should; and while we
shall consider it almost exclusively from the
emotional standpoint, as one of the main-
springs of human behaviour, I maintain that
we cannot do so to any purpose without a full
recognition of it as an *Abstract Principle* which
is inherent, innate, and of supreme value as a
plastic force in the hands of man.

This might be called for the sake of distinction a purely "human" view, one aiming to get
at the heart of the subject as nearly as possible in its relation to the daily lives of men and
women; yet even here the number of laws to
be deduced is few, and any frank discussion of
personal sex-problems being somewhat beyond
the scope of this work, it is very difficult to

convey that knowledge which the author feels to be of paramount importance in the treatment of Behaviour.

The only available Psychology of Sex up to date, beyond the observations of men like Herbert Spencer and Havelock Ellis, and the scattered work of the modern novelists, is that to be found in the recent but extensive studies in mental Pathology. The Pathology of Sex is extremely valuable, throwing as it does much needed illumination on the hitherto hidden phases of the normal healthy sex-life.

A knowledge of life that does not include a certain degree of information on this subject is not only incomplete, but is seriously hampered. Only by some acquaintance with the appalling and widespread degeneracies of Sex, for instance, can one gain any perspective of its mysterious power, as well as the criminal ignorance which surrounds it on all sides. Studies such as these if carried to any extent may, of course, produce morbid reactions of a harmful character and should be undertaken only by a mature and well-balanced mind or under proper direction; for it is not difficult when peering for long into these abysses to lose one's faith in the real wholesomeness and stability of human beings.

As for any belief in the essential *purity* of Sex, needless to say it cannot be found in the fields of Pathology, and to tarry too long therein may deprive one of that which one already has. Yet I see no hope for the future of humanity without that kind and quality of courage which fears nothing, not even the depravity before which human nature so often lies abject. To *see* is to remedy, mayhap—at least we can do nothing with our eyes bandaged and our hands tied.

I have just said that the study of Sexual Pathology should be undertaken only by the mature and serious-minded—this is true enough, but if we were only big enough and clear enough in our own minds about the entire subject of Sex to educate our children properly, the whole problem of Sexual Pathology would shortly be solved, or very nearly so. For the harm begins with our unwillingness to answer the natural questions of the child when they first arise in his consciousness. We hate to admit—for reasons inexplicable, except perhaps for shame at our own failure to solve the problem—the appearance of the Sex-instinct in the child. As a matter of course it first develops at about five years of age—last probably in the chronology of the instincts—and it is at this period that the child first begins his natural inquiries, which are destined to be met with such lies and evasions as to finally discourage him and turn back upon himself the rising currents of his most vital energies.

What untold harm is generated at this point there is no computing; but certain it is that none but the most favoured child escapes the discord and marring incident upon such an experience. And when I say favoured, I mean either that child born of such parents that he is reared in both freedom and wisdom, or that still more unusual one who is of such temperamental *soundness* as to escape unscathed, by miracle as it were, from the psychological mires and tangles thus imposed upon him.

Why is it that parents evade this plain duty, this one path more vital to the welfare of their children than any other? It is not because they are entirely without knowledge, for life has taught it to them, usually with much pain and many scars. It is not because they are afraid of "putting the wrong thoughts into the children's minds" for they know quite well what the right ones are. They have only to look back into their own childhood to know that in the absence of the right attitude and instruction from the parents, the child will inevitably satisfy his curiosity in channels that are sure to be saturated with poison. No, it is none of these things, it is simply *cowardice,* a dread of facing facts that are too big for them and an unwillingness to rise superior to the lethargy and silence imposed by custom.

Probably this reluctance has its origin in an acquired dislike and desire to repress what is felt to be only an "animal instinct"—somehow with the development of the Intellect has come a breaking away from natural standards and a heady sort of contempt for conditions which at an earlier stage of our evolution were accepted simply enough. It is not natural, it is not sensible, and it is not right, to assume an attitude of *moral superiority* toward Sex or any other vital fact of life. And yet we do it.

I believe a study of Natural Science in the early years of life would do much to dissipate the prudish and harmful feeling about "animal instincts." Children born and raised in the country where they see the natural life of animals are more apt to be normal in their attitude toward certain primitive facts, but even they could gain a new and deeper significance by the wider and more thoughtful observation to be obtained through scientific studies. Less time spent upon dead languages and impertinent mathematical problems and more upon obtaining knowledge of the vital human processes would do much to eradicate the false and shallow ignorance so prevalent today. It would do much to save the innocent, weak, and as-

piring children who are set out upon life's way
in utter ignorance of its manifold dangers and
pitfalls.

It is true there has been a certain amount
of modern agitation for sex-education in
the schools, which has resulted in hopeful
attempts in this direction. They are, however,
perfunctory, in the nature of the circumstances;
and the duty (and incidentally the privilege)
falls back upon the parent, who is after all the
only one who can speak of the finer and more
intimate phases of Sex with the proper delicacy.

But to successfully teach anything about Sex
to either young or old, we must first strip it
of some of the many misconceptions surrounding it. Having disposed of the folly of our
habit of silence in connection with it and of the
fallacious attitude which sees in it something
intrinsically low and ignoble, let us now consider
the important question of the true *function* of
the sex-principle, as it shows itself in the physical relations of men and women.

There has always been a strong contingent
insisting upon the purely racial functions of

Sex and who believe that it exists only for the perpetuity of the race without respect to individual desires or welfare. It has been contended that Nature, the blind force bent upon multiplication and continuity, brings each pair together with the single ulterior design of uniting them for reproductive purposes.

The universality and seeming inevitability of the law of reproduction gives some ground, of course, for such a claim; but if we as human beings have been endowed with Reason, and Will, and Emotions, and if, furthermore, we have come into any degree of spiritual self-consciousness, what can it all be for if not to declare our rights as individuals in matters so pertinent as these?

What can be of greater importance than the personal sex-life? Yet we have been taught that an absolute resignation and obeisance to the universal laws is necessary in this, while endeavouring with serious purpose to free ourselves from other conditions no less universal and apparently as inevitable. We do not spare any effort to overcome sickness and disease, for instance, and to save all forms of human life, even those that are defective or useless alike to society and to themselves. Yet any discussion of "birth-control" or possible checks to population is met with a storm of protest and cries of "race-suicide."

From a sociological standpoint even the senile decadence and death of the individual may be shown to be advantageous to the race, but it would certainly be odd to describe this as advantageous to the individual. Certain physical feelings plainly lead to the propagation of the species, but this does not help us at all to ascertain what unknown character and significance they may have as sources of expression and fulfilment for the individual.

To suppose for a moment that the majority of people meet in a physical union for the specific purpose of reproduction, or to satisfy their parental feelings, is sheer folly; and to sidestep the question by assuming that this function was made desirable simply to maintain the race, is equally fallacious, reducing the whole matter to a purely mechanical device, eliminating every one of its psychical, emotional, and spiritual elements.

The error lies in placing Sex among the inevitable fatalities of life and then endeavouring to find suitable explanations that will enable us to submit gracefully to a force which apparently we cannot escape. Quite apart from its undeniable collective social purpose, we should frankly recognize that it is intended, in its higher phases, to augment and sustain the individual—to serve man rather than enslave him.

Let us briefly trace the evolution of Sex from its early or instinctive state. In the majority of animals and in some men it does not rise above the level of a mere physical sensation, blind and insistent; even in beings devoid of nervous systems, as in the vegetable or animal micro-organisms, we find the same law at work. The equivalent of sexual attraction is even to be found in the mineral world in the chemical selective affinity plainly apparent between certain atoms. In man this instinct evinces itself as a semi-conscious appetite, a hunger, driving him by its force to seek satisfaction as best he may

and in much the same manner as he obtains food
for the body.

Rising from the realm of simple physical
impulse Sex becomes an Emotion, an Idea,
where instead of being a blind isolated force,
it becomes a conscious and complex desire,
united in varying measure to all the finest
instincts in human nature. We have already
considered what the power of untrammeled
Emotion may be and can realize that the Sex-
emotion, especially, requires for its higher expression a tempering by, and coalescence with,
the Will. When this point is reached we have
a truly spiritual impulse, containing and in-
cluding in itself the whole range of human expression.

When once we appreciate the exalted
heights to which Sex as a force may attain,
we can better understand that the opposite end
of this pole of possibilities must be as low as
the one is high. In other words the depths of
infamy to which the human manifestations of
Sex have descended are but measures of the
magnificent heights to which it may reach.

The degree of these possibilities and this development are solely dependent upon the individual. In so far as he can personally realize the depth and significance of the Sex-feeling, in so far can he elevate himself and the race. To begin with, he must know that Sex is mental and spiritual as well as physical; he must see the sex-act not only in its utilitarian aspect but as a *symbol* of the *great creative act* by which all life came into being. He must recognize himself as a Conscious Creator; not only a creator in the physical sense, contributing his quota to the world's population; but as a generator of force, magnetism, of ideas and emotional power, which when once conceived and released are undoubtedly the greatest contributions any one human being can make to life.

It may be a new idea to many that the generation of either mental or emotional power has anything to do with Sex or with the sex-relation. The thought of it as existing solely for the satisfaction of a physical need has been adhered to so closely that its connection with and

instigation of the higher mental and emotional
processes has been for the most part overlooked.

It is true of course that both ideas and emotional power can be formed and projected by
one individual alone, and quite apart from the
sex-act, although even then the process is essentially a generative one; but when two people
come together who are in any sense mated, there
is not only an exchange of their respective
qualities, there is also the creation of something new, a power, a third element which represents the sum total and combination of all
their energies and attributes.

This is true to some extent even when
there is no conscious sex-feeling between
them, as in the case of friends; but the
greater the intimacy the greater the possibilities; and the something new that is created becomes the joint possession of both. When it
is a physical union *only* that takes place, the
natural outcome is a physical conception, the
production of another human being; when the
contact is on one of the higher planes also,

there may be in addition, or instead of, the usual physical outcome, a conception and birth of new powers, new visions—an *im-material* fruition it is true, but who shall say that it is not of at least equal import, if not greater?

The generative process when thus ethereal-ized may perhaps no longer be called *genera-tion;* but it can be called *regeneration,* in that it "makes over" the persons participating in it and transmutes a physical impulse into an ex-hilarating experience that co-ordinates and blends the entire nature. It involves the con-scious sublimation of an instinct, which though intrinsically good, has hitherto been very lim-ited in its expression; and it opens the door on some of those hidden springs of creative energy which animate us all at times. It tends also to bring under the control of the conscious Will a force that is ordinarily only intermittent in its manifestation.

The reason of all this is not far to seek. Again we see the quality of Nature expressing itself, this time in the *positive* and *negative* elements as represented by man and woman. Each possesses certain inherent qualities which complement and fulfil those of the other. Man is simple, dominant, his natural occupations those of the forager and provider—woman is complex and receptive, her functions those of tending, giving form and direction to that which is supplied her. These characteristics are general, though a gradual fusion is to be noted as taking place between the sexes which points to an extension of the capacities of both men and women until each is all-inclusive and self-sufficient. This does not necessarily imply a complete absorption of one in the other and a consequent loss of their separate characteristics. The *Androgyne,* toward which I feel we are tending, will not be a sexless creature, but a more complete one, thus making the process of give and take between men and women one of infinitely greater potentialities that at present.

While the male is to all appearances the stronger and more dominant of the two sexes, this is true on the external plane only. Psychically the relations of the two are reversed, and as between them woman becomes the positive element, the leader.

A common misconception is that women are more apathetic and weaker sexually than men. As a matter of fact they are much less passive sexually than is generally supposed and should be given credit for the same primary endowment that we assume quite naturally belongs to man. There are, of course, a considerable number of women of markedly cold natures, even among women who are not only intelligent and capable, but attractive to the opposite sex; but this is one of the variations and abnormalities incident upon a certain type and does not apply at all to women in general.

Not only is the normal woman well-sexed, but she is capable by reason of greater imagination and sensitiveness, of expressing her sex-feelings in stronger, finer and more varied ways than a man. She possesses what most men do not, a power of *diffusion,* so that passion is not to her a thing concentrated only in the sex-act but a force capable of inspiring all kinds of deep emotion, especially that of affectionate and maternal regard. A woman's mate is to her always somewhat of a child— which is as it should be, since most men never outgrow boyhood even in their maturity.

The presence of the more delicate and intuitive sides of a woman's nature fit her in a peculiar way to be the leader, if not the aggressor, in the sex-relation. This is quite contrary to the conventional opinion which assumes that a woman's part is always, or should be, that of passivity or acquiescence, that it is not "womanly" to permit even the faintest sign of her natural desire to show itself. Nothing could be more absurd or contrary to nature, since the primary law in regard to the relation of the sexes is that it is a matter concerning each alike, a partnership, an expression of equality. The spontaneity of such an attitude has of course been much disturbed or destroyed by the property rights vested in man and his assumption of possession or ownership of the woman.

As a matter of fact, and fortunately for the

happiness and good of the race, women have
more or less evaded this imposition, by the development of subtlety and *finesse*.   If this tendency becomes at times sheer craftiness, it is but
an expression of the law of compensation, an
inevitable reaction from too much pressure and
constraint.   By means of her subtlety and intuition, woman more often than not leads, if
she does not control man, in all the varied relations which in the natural course consummate
themselves in a sex-union or marriage.   She is
quicker, more perceptive, and unconsciously
takes advantage of man's lesser knowledge of
himself, and of his general inarticulateness.

The pity is that this superiority is not usually
maintained after marriage—then, something apparently innate in the woman, a certain weakness and tendency to slavishness, betrays her.
She becomes abject under the power of her
emotions and bestows herself without reserve.
Nothing is more fatal to the permanance and
pleasure of the relationship—not because of
anything innately ignoble in the man, but because the woman has abdicated her natural po-

sition of prophetess and guide into those mysterious realms which are always better known to her than to her mate.

Also in the exercise of her power of elective affinity, she has deprived the man of his equally strong desire to *seek*—in fact, as his affection and attentions very largely centre around himself as "quester," this quality must be fostered and not smothered by his mate. He knows instinctively that the woman's knowledge and feeling is finer and deeper than his—with this she must content herself.

All men of fine feeling recognize this difference and would prefer that a woman maintain at least a degree of aloofness, not more than is compatible with ardent and loving expressions to be sure, but enough to permit him to feel that he still retains his own freedom and individuality, as well as to allow him the possession of a certain Ideal to which he may look for guidance.

All of these delicacies and interrelations of Sex are quite missed ordinarily because the conventional point of view is so firmly fixed upon the man as a "lord of creation" and the woman as his "serf." That this unfortunate inequality has prevailed for the most part for ages past does not mean that, in spite of an outward seeming, many have not come much nearer to the true secrets of Sex than would have been supposed; and where today the relationship is still so often one of inequality, of master and slave, we must not forget that when such is the case it is quite as much the fault of the acquiescing, self-immolating woman as it is of the egotistic and dominating male.

Both sexes have yet much to learn—there is great hope in the comparative freedom between them that is more customary today, especially in America, than probably ever before. If we can develop a true co-operation and better sense of *camaraderie,* we will have paved the way toward that ideal union of which we all dream. In that day men will cease their *patronage* of women, women will cease their machinations for the enmeshing of men. Sex will be in a fair way to become the constructive

personal element it was meant to be, as well
as the great upbuilder of the race.

To better arrive at the personal possibilities
in Sex, let us outline again more definitely its
several planes of expression. On the physical
plane we have the whole problem of generation, which through the modern science of
Eugenics has been given some small part of the
attention it deserves. We study zealously in
order to master every detail of the law of reproduction when we wish to breed cattle or
other fine animals, and definite specific results
are secured, showing how far man has progressed in his mastery of these physical laws.
Certainly the production of the human species
is of infinitely greater importance than the
breeding of animals, though the present trend in
this direction confines itself so closely to the
purely mechanical and physical side of the question as to be very limited in its value.

In order to have vigorous and well endowed
offspring, men and women have many other
problems to consider than the merely physical
ones. The conception of a child should be a

sacrament; which implies not only a high intention, but has even more to do with mind and soul
states than it has with the body.   When this is
understood, and not before, our children will
be the outcome of our highest and most complete selves and worthy of our best desires.

It seems in this connection almost unnecessary to call attention to that view which regards
the physical sex-craving as a law unto itself.
Yet there are many still bound by it, especially
among men, who having always claimed "freedom" to satisfy this appetite, know comparatively little of the possibilities and advantages
of restraint.   Too often does the man prepare
the funeral of his own pleasure either through a
degrading promiscuity, or by attempting to exercise a mastership over his partner rather
than over himself.   In nothing is he more likely
to be selfish and yet nothing will deprive him
more quickly or completely of the possibility of
an adequate response from his mate.

Clearly no man has the moral right to enter
into the marriage relation without having first
demonstrated to himself that he is a master of

his physical feelings and capable of self-control.
Many there are who possess these virtues in
other fields and yet neglect them sadly in the
most important relationship in life and thus
destroy the finest and best that would otherwise
be in store for them. There are women too who
need this caution, women who though they may
display it in somewhat different ways, yet tinge
all their behaviour with an unmastered sex-instinct.

Another phase of the physical side of Sex is
the constructive one it affords of an opportunity for the exchange of magnetism or bodily
vibrations. Though it is not possible to separate these entirely from vibrations characteristic of the mental and emotional life, we all
know the physical magnetism and power of the
human "touch" and the pleasure it gives us
merely to be near certain people. This sensation arises from the stimulus of harmonious
vibrations and where the sex-element in it is
strong it can be exceedingly invigourating and
salubrious.

To make the interchange of any value, the

magnetic output between the two must be nearly equalized; otherwise we see the common phenomenon of one of the pair waxing strong at the expense of the other. Physical intercourse should augment the strength of both parties to it and in the absence of this some important readjustment is required between them.

In the emotional realm of Sex there is the greatest possible range and it is the one most widely experienced, in spite of the commonly-held idea that Sex is entirely physical. The emotionalism of Sex is only partially understood, and the Freudian contention that *all* emotions are associated with the sex-emotion has raised a storm of protest; but this is only because the universal significance of Sex is not yet comprehended.

The sex-feeling has, emotionally, two principal functions. It is at the same time the greatest *outlet* and the greatest *stimulus* of which we have any knowledge. It is in the nature of a tonic—simply to feel that one is desired, and attractive in the eyes of the opposite sex is a great exhilaration. This feeling is especially strong in women who often covet admiration that they never wish to see realized or consummated in any way. They are satisfied and thrive upon the simple stimulus of having aroused an attraction or desire in another. This emotion extends all the way from the most innocent and unconscious flirtation or "passing attraction," to a state of vampirism or deliberate exercise of sex-power for the enslavement of another.

If all sex-emotion is repressed, the result is either irritability and extreme sensitiveness, or great depression and lack of vitality. If excessive it satiates and weakens, though the danger on this score is comparatively small, except where there is no natural check as in cases of solitary indulgence.

Many and serious pathological states result from a misuse of the sex-emotion, especially from a long continued abstinence, even in those of a very normal and equable temperament. An extended deprivation in either sex, for whatever reason, is productive of all sorts of

mental, moral, nervous, and physical disorders.
Compensating factors may be provided, of
course, to ameliorate the intensity of the symptoms; congenial friends, creative occupation,
and outdoor life do much to maintain the disturbed equilibrium; but the fact still remains,
however much we may dislike to admit it, that
the complete abstinence from both physical and
emotional sex elements is abnormal and brings
its own penalty.

Physicians know this but can do little, as ordinarily the only advice they can give is impracticable and apt to be anti-social in its application.   The problem is manifestly one for treatment by the Psycho-therapist, who if he cannot remedy the lack in his patient's life, can at
least offer him some reasonable substitutes in
the way of mental and emotional expressions.

A gentle stimulus of the sex-emotion is
gained through all normal social intercourse,
and especially in such amusements as dancing,
where the magnetic exchanges are secured as
well.   Any segregation of the sexes that is long
continued cannot be otherwise than detrimen-

tal. It is particularly desirable that during the adolescent period there should be a free intermingling, in spite of the distractions and loss of mental interests that is often claimed as a result of association in this period. The "old maid" who lives in a family of brothers or masculine friends seldom develops the peculiarities so characteristic of her in an isolated state. Men lose not only their charm and gentleness of manner when much separated from women but suffer other depletions as well.

Theoretically the association of man and wife is supposed to supply all the needed elements; as a matter of fact the relationship is seldom ideal enough to make this fully practicable, and the line therefore that has been drawn around married people is both arbitrary and harmful to their best interests. A free interchange of social pleasures between both the married and the unmarried is essential to any degree of emotional balance. The alleged dangers lying in these associations are little enough in comparison to the richness to be gained through the added variety and freedom.

Many and subtle are the elements drawing men and women together, but none is so potent and inclusive as that of *sex-love*—a relation, by the way, which is comparatively recent in the history of the world, at least in the ideal sense in which we now conceive it. Let us analyze it a little, and we find its *nucleus* to be the attraction or fascination usually called "physical" for lack of any better name. It is, of course, the great animating sex-principle, without which *love* is a mere shadow. Let us see now what emotions are most closely associated with and built upon this centre.

To begin with there is the sentiment which we term *Affection*, a feeling that must be regarded as an independent sentiment, as it can exist between those of the same sex; but one which in the love-relation is greatly exalted. It leads to tenderness, consideration and a desire to conserve the happiness of the one loved.

Sex-love also awakens a feeling for *personal beauty* which includes a whole set of valuable and pleasurable emotions. Particularly is this true of the feeling entertained by men for the

women they love, which is as it should be since
women's especial function is to represent the
real principle of beauty. A man hitherto quite
unconscious of the existence of beauty, finds
himself aroused to a whole new series of perceptions under the influence of a sex attraction.

All love that is worthy of the name includes
the sentiments of *admiration, respect,* or *reverence.* These also are feelings which may exist
outside Sex but which in this relation become
in a high degree active. In the more intellectualized forms of love it is quite impossible for
the sex-feeling to exist except in conjunction
with sincere admiration or even adulation; and
who has not revelled in the love of approbation
that is thus satisfied! Being preferred above
all others and by that one admired above all
others, affords the deepest gratification possible and lends a real support. Furthermore, to
have succeeded in gaining such attachment
from and sway over another is a proof of
power and attractiveness which cannot fail to
increase and sustain one's self-esteem. Nothing so elevates a man in his own opinion as to

have secured a response from the woman he values above all others.

A common attribute of sex-love is the *proprietary* feeling, the pleasure of possession, the belonging to each other. Sometimes this emotion is so strong as to make for selfish isolation, a state particularly noticeable in the first beginnings of the relation and one which if indulged in too much soon destroys itself. It also nurses foolish jealousies and sometimes bondage and tyranny.

This sense of "belonging," however, is closely allied to the extended sympathetic perception that comes from being able to unite one's self so closely with another. All pleasures are doubled by another's sympathetic companionship, all sorrows assuaged by the same sense of sharing—it leads to, and has in it the possibilities of the finest kind of comradeship. There may even be a real mental affinity, though this seldom develops in a like degree with the emotional one.

That real companionship is seldom attained in marriage is not due to an intrinsic barrier

in the relation, but to a lack of knowledge and
appreciation of its true possibilities. Undoubtedly the greatest pleasure in a true
union is the intoxication ensuing upon the
demolition of the barriers that naturally surround each human being. The greater the intimacy the greater the concessions required, yet
the sense of thus acquiring a greater liberty of
action, of crossing the subtle boundaries which
may not ordinarily be crossed, affords an intense gratification and relief from the feeling
of personal isolation which for ever enfolds us.

Beside and beyond all these feelings, there
is at the root of all love-attractions and attach-
ments, the unconscious *search for an ideal*, the
quest of each soul for its mate, its completion
and fulfilment. The hope is always that these
wants may be realized in a single individual and
throughout a whole lifetime—an ideal which
puts a heavy responsibility, whether he will or
no, on every person presuming to enter such
a relationship.

Much of the unhappiness in marriage
might be avoided if so much were not ex-

pected of it—if we could find somewhere
the golden mean between excessive exactions
and a demoralizing laxness. We long so much
to concretize and personalize our Ideal that we
forget that no one human being can be perfect
enough to fulfil it. Yet the emotion which in-
spires this search and thus dramatizes a real
spiritual need is of the finest and should be
safeguarded accordingly.

To destroy faith and trust by a conscious be-
trayal is universally conceded to be a heinous
sin and opposed in its very nature to the in-
tegrity which is the foundation of all love and
friendship. But what is much more common,
though less recognized, is the pain and disappointment consequent upon the failure of the
loved one to live up to the expectations he or
she originally created. However unreasonable
it may be, it is a fact that more tragedies hang
upon this unsatisfied desire than upon anything
else in life. Perhaps in time, with a better
emotional education, greater tolerance, and
freer social conditions, we will be able to heal
this demoralizing sorrow.

Occasionally we see love relations between the sexes that are entirely devoid of the sexual element, that is, in its recognized physical form. Owing to the comparative freedom from conflict and intensity, there is a certain quiet comradeship to be obtained from such a union not unlike that between friends of the same sex; but there is no question that it lacks the sparkle and effervescence of the more complete union that has as its basis an expression of the creative fires.

The distinctions between the *emotional* and the *psychical* phases of Sex are clear enough to the Psychologist but too subtle and intricate to be considered in detail here. Suffice it to say that the more attenuated and penetrating intermingling that takes place between two sensitives on the psychical plane establishes a more perfect polarity and represents the progression of Sex into higher and still higher phases. Between people who have been intimately connected there is a subtle alliance created that persists, as though they were for ever present each with the other. It is the indication of a greater degree of unity, though it does not always represent *harmony*. It may lead to the most exquisite delight or it may produce unutterable torture.

The difference lies in whether the psychical closeness is supplemented by all the other elements in the nature—if not, great discord is an almost certain result. It is possible, for instance, to find unity in a *physical* intercourse that does not include any other elements, and it is even possible to find points of *emotional* contact which are sufficient in themselves; but when the plane of *psychical* contact is reached, the capacity of the participants is greatly extended and it is with great difficulty that one can escape its bonds.

For this reason the greatest care should be taken that no psychic coalition should take place, unless one has absolute trust and confidence in one's mate, as well as a protecting measure of self-sufficiency. For it is like the mingling of liquids, once combined their identity is lost, they cannot again be withdrawn into their respective selves—at least not without an elaborate process of mental alchemy not known to many.

We often observe great friction and incompatibility between people whose nearness to each other can be nothing but an irritation and pain; yet they seem quite unable to effect the separation that the circumstances would seem to require. We are often witness to attractions of so violent a nature that they are in effect repulsions and yet the bond still holds. We can only conclude that somewhere in the nature a hold has been gained, and a psychic fusion consummated, which proves an irresistible obstacle for the Will. Some hidden element is being satisfied even though everything in the conscious life is at war with it.

Psychic unity often extends to the transference of mental and physical qualities from one to the other, and occasionally disturbing physical symptoms are also transmitted so that each member of the pair becomes ill if the other is affected. Strange presentiments arise in relation to the one who may chance to be absent, and not infrequently his or her mental state, or even actions, may be photographed vividly on the mind of the other. All of these phenomena occur, at times, under other circumstances than those connected with physical intercourse, but they are nevertheless augmented by and very largely the result of commingling sex-forces.

Another phase of the psychical union is the stimulation it affords the Imagination. Under proper and balanced conditions a stimulation of sex-passion will greatly increase the fecundity of the imagination—thus are produced many of our finest works of art, music, and literature, all of which are *creations,* pure expressions of Sex. The transference of various talents may be deliberately effected in this manner by the initiated, so that a quite unproductive person may suddenly give signs of the acquisition of new powers and capacities, such as writing poetry or accomplishing any other creative labour with unusual dispatch and ability.

The dangers of psychical sex-expression without any accompanying physical interchange have already been touched upon in the

chapter on Imagination. The strange behaviour of many poor unfortunates is all clearly
accounted for when we understand the strong
tendency of the Imagination to dwell upon
erotic impulses, especially when deprived or
limited in other ways.

All intellectual companionships are the expression of Sex on the mental plane. They are
equally possible and even more common between
those of the same sex as of the opposite one,
the brain being in one case characteristically
positive, in the other negative, irrespective of
whether it is in a feminine or a masculine body.
The combination of complementary forces on
this plane is most stimulating and helpful, it
is the basis of all real friendship and affords
an opportunity not only for an exchange of
ideas but actually creates and produces ideas.
"Platonic" friendships come in this class, often
affording a real satisfaction, though each one
of them naturally contains the seeds of a more
frankly sexual relationship and thus supplies,
in addition, a certain zest, if not danger, to
those concerned in it.

The presence of a strongly creative nature in an intellectual company is sure to show itself by an emission of sparks from the mind, which tends to stimulate and draw a response from all those present. For this reason we are much better able to express ourselves in the presence of certain people than of others; ease takes the place of embarrassment when the creative forces are working well on the mental plane between those concerned. All intellectual achievements are the fruit of the hidden sex-life and represent a transmutation of creative energy from the physical to the mental plane.

Sometimes this transfer may be so complete as to leave one physically depleted. While the strongly intellectual nature is not necessarily cold, it often appears so by reason of the constant and habitual sublimation of its sex-force into more attenuated forms. As between men and women a strongly intellectual attachment does not as a rule demonstrate itself on the physical-emotional plane and vice versa—though, of course, the ideal for which we all strive is the complete unity of the two.

It only remains to speak of the *soul-union*, that strange and intoxicating transmission of the life-force that takes place between those who can meet on the spiritual plane. That such an achievement may be the direct outcome of a sex-union is among the secrets known only to those whose personal development has allowed them a glimpse of another plane of experience, a state of consciousness which approaches the cosmic.

In its quality and extent every form of aspiration is the expression of a sex-yearning and in no better way can this realization of the superior forces of the universe be attained than through the spiritual union of aspiring lovers. Each carries, or gives, all that he has, or is, to the other. Each finds in the soul of his mate a certain completion for himself—indeed so complete is the absorption in a mystical union of this kind that the sense of self is entirely lost. There is a melting away of *all* the barriers and something of the meaning of universality and transcendence is at least momentarily realized. It is the contention of some

that such a union precludes the need of, or desire for, any contact on the physical plane, but
except in extremely isolated cases, I see no
signs as yet of our having outgrown the need
and advantage of our physical selves. Sex is
a force that lends lustre to all it touches—if it
can glorify the mind and soul, why not the
body also?

The solution of the ever perplexing Sex problem must of necessity be a personal one. There
is no question but that the existing social order
combats nature's greatest passion vigorously
and relentlessly—more bruises, pains, sacri-
fices, and tragedies are exacted of us here than
anywhere. We feel the need of guarding this
instinct—and we guard it so fiercely as to very
nearly destroy ourselves. We hate *repression* and we fear *freedom*—but between the two
we oscillate and strangle. We object to and see
the folly of the "double standard," yet we are
afraid of its only alternative—a greater freedom for women—knowing full well that man
will not relinquish such as he already possesses. We crave a means of limiting off-

spring and saving our women some of the bur-
dens of excessive child-bearing—yet we dread
the dissemination of the knowledge that would
make this possible.   We feel that woman should
have a free and untrammelled choice of her
mate, yet we hedge her about with every pre-
caution and restraint, discourage her free
association with men, and provide her with
no means of economic independence. We
shrink lest the taint of some sexual "perver-
sion" or unmentionable disease shall touch us
or those near to us, yet we sedulously secrete
any knowledge we may possess on the subject,
leading our children and young people to the
very doors of fate and resigning them to it with
scarce a qualm as to their utter and helpless
ignorance.

All these are social problems of the gravest
import, about which the widest divergence of
opinion is held.   But may the day be hastened
when we can attack these things fearlessly and
strip Sex of the whole mass of conditions which
are not truly germane to it—the day when
women will be permitted more than the one

virtue of sex-chastity, and when they are eman-
cipated from an undesired maternity; when
homo-sexuality, however unfortunate, is known
to be neither a crime nor a disease; when even
marriage and divorce will not be matters of
public grace or disgrace, but entirely personal
voluntary concerns; when the economic changes
that are agitating the world today shall have re-
solved themselves into constructive and stable
elements; and especially when women shall have
been accorded the position of dignity and independence which they are now showing signs of
being ready to fill—in that day truly we will
be in sight of the millennium.

Let us do our part in preparation for it by
realizing that the Sex-instinct is the centre
around which everything revolves, that nothing exists but through it. Sex is the great de-
veloper of character, the great motive power
behind work and play alike—activity of every
sort. It lends strength to the Will, it warms
and colours life with all that is beautiful and
good. It is likewise the root of all religious
feeling, in that it expresses the search for the

ideal and an aspiration for the highest ends to which man can reach, either in fact or in imagination. It is *The Force*—let us by so recognizing it fortify and prepare ourselves to grapple with and master it.

CHAPTER VII

SELF

THE PSYCHOLOGY OF THE EGO

HUMAN beings, outside of their physical bodies and simple mental attributes, are elusive, difficult to account for—with all our analysis there is always a mysterious x somewhere in the composition that seems to escape our most careful dissections. And pure science permits of the introduction of no mysticism into its sacred precincts—there all must be verifiable, proven, reduced to "facts." This is all necessary enough as a method and when confined to certain domains or departments of human research, but it gives us no grasp at all when we come to look for some unifying element, the background or substance which we feel *must* lie behind all psychological phenomena. We seek reality—above all, we seek it in ourselves, in that spiritual entity forming the core of every life—but we do not find it in Science.

We can only search within our own consciousness for what is "behind"—and in some fortui-
tous moments we are rewarded with a flash, an
illuminating glimpse of that string upon which
all the beads of our personality are hung. It
is the Self, the indissoluble Ego, the Essence of
all being.

In a vague way man is always *aware* of
himself, but his *sense of Self* increases gradually in proportion to his development until he
recognizes an inner identity so permanent and
cohesive as to withstand all the invasions and
mutations of life and experience. So strong
is this feeling that in most cases he is conscious
of a great longing for, if not a certitude of, an
indefinite continuation of himself in time. Belief in personal immortality is as old as the
human race itself and as ineradicable, despite a
discouraging lack of "proof."

The *"I"* which constitutes the pivot of the
universe for each one of us, is an indivisible
monad, possessing an unchanging and inde-
structible nature of its own. Around it are
grouped many thoughts and feelings of vary-

ing proportion and quality in each human being, accretions that in their entirety make up the character or personality. We know the *"I"* as the basis, a reality, apart from the *contents of the mind.* We are conscious of perceptions, emotions, volitions, *etc.,* but as compared with the Self, these things are objective and mere accumulations. They may be said to constitute *"Personality"* however, or the acquired qualities upon which *Behaviour* so largely depends.

Personality is a universal characteristic shared in some degree by every one, it is subject to mutation and variation, and it can be *developed.* The very origin of the word "personal" indicates something assumed or put on, designating as it did the masks worn by the actors in the ancient plays. Personality is the colour, or dress, as it were, of the Ego. It varies according to the plane of development of the Ego and also changes with each experience; but it should not be confused with *Individuality,* which expresses the *innateness* of character or the essence of selfhood.

Individuality is dependent on the *timbre* or vibratory quality that distinguishes each of us from the other and is not perceptibly altered throughout a lifetime, although we have reason to believe that it, too, is a living, growing thing, capable of infinite development. *Personality* is dependent upon many things—ancestry, influence of family and environment, intelligence, education, ideals, experience, physical semblance, manners—all go to make up a something which is too ethereal to define, yet which is clearly perceived by every one. It is a composite and fluid thing—and it expands as one's consciousness spreads out from the physical self to its appurtenances. One's clothes, manners and dwelling place are, for instance, an expression of one's personality; and the same may be said of one's friends, fortune, business, club, church and country.

The trouble is that we take such a superficial view of life as a rule that we fail to see the inner life at all, either of others or ourselves. We should be able to pierce the outer coverings, not only such externalities as physical appearance, manner and dress, but even those mental guises assumed quite unconsciously by all of us. How often we are deceived by that which appears to be virtue, only to prove itself the very opposite. How seldom can we recognize and judge rightly of those soul qualities which alone distinguish a man for what he is rather than for what he seems to be. We are sadly in need of more thought and reflection as to the true nature of the Self and its function as the ultimate director of all our destinies.

In some measure all are possessed of a *self-feeling,* but the real consciousness of Self comes only with maturity of mind and soul. The self-feeling pure and simple is an intellectualized form of the instinct of conservation—it is man at the point in his development where reflection first enters in to make him aware of his strength or weakness, or what he feels to be such. By providing him with a consciousness of his powers it permits him somewhat of a true measure of his pretensions, so that his ambitions do not too far outrun his ability to materialize them.

The self-feeling is developed first through contact with our fellow men and especially through the intercourse afforded by language. Without language we should be mutually exclusive and impenetrable. With it each mind transcends its own limits and shares the minds of others. This enables one to gain a perspective of one's self and is therefore the beginning of the self-feeling as well as the social feeling.

In the higher states this mental contact is enhanced by the development of intuition and the various forms of psychic intercommunication that it affords—all of which serves under normal circumstances to increase the consciousness of Self. Unless very fundamental and well-developed however, the self-feeling is dependent on the *approbation of others* and is impaired by criticism or fear of blame. This is the mark of the undeveloped Ego and the cause of much weakness and unhappiness. A comfortable feeling of self-sufficiency accompanies a true *amour-propre*, which implies that the Ego is a well organized unit and not to be disturbed by externalities.

The self-feeling has two clearly defined forms, the positive one which may be called *pride,* leading to strength, courage, and aggression. The negative form, or *humility,* leads mostly to weakness and impotence but is nevertheless an expression of the consciousness of Self. Courage is man's greatest virtue, Nietzsche has told us; and as its very foundation is this same *sense of Self,* it is plain to see the reason of the difference in the attack made by different people upon life. But true courage as well as true unselfishness grows out of a recognition of the "I" rather than the "me"—it is impersonal, not personal.

In its excessive or pathological forms the self-feeling becomes anti-social and destructive in its nature, forming some of the many well defined disturbances of the personality. When it is an exaggeration of the importance of the self (the little one, not the big one) it is called *megalomania* and leads to ruthlessness and cruelty. Or it may take the apparently negative but equally destructive form of *self-pity,* a desire to attract attention by playing upon the sympathy or tenderness of others.

The personality is indeed subject to many diseases. The widespread "mental-nervous" afflictions of the day are all derangements of the personality, due mostly to the high living and great waste of vitality which is characteristic of our race and time—all making for "nervousness" or disintegration. There are other causes more obscure and fundamental, having to do with the incarnation of the Ego in its physical body. Even in persons who appear quite normal this occult process is sometimes incomplete, making any thorough co-ordination between the several planes of expression difficult or impossible. Even such intricate problems as this can be overcome, however, by certain methods of re-integration on the psychic plane.

The greatest danger to the personality is that of *dissociation*. In its extreme form we have multiple or alternating personalities, where one phase emerges with such strength and vividness as to temporarily, or perhaps for a long period of time, entirely eclipse the others. The chapter on Repressions suggested some of the most frequent causes of this pathological condition, but a quite common and normal cause arises from the tendency inherent in all of us to show only single phases of ourselves to different people. Thus one friend draws out the gay and flippant side, another knows us only as serious and philosophical, still another may arouse a subconscious resentment or antagonism, while in the presence of certain people we are sure to be both thoughtful and tender. These variations are inevitable of course, and lend both colour and charm to life; but if each aspect is too long continued in its separate groove, we are apt to have a phase of dissociation which may result disastrously. Thus a man who is persistently of one type and character in his business relations may in the bosom of his family show quite another self— too often a less attractive one, I fear.

Disintegration is the logical outcome of *dissociation* and other negative disturbances of the personality. In its most serious and final form it results in insanity or suicide. All the stages from simple day-dreaming and fits of "abstraction" to violent madness are but disturbances of the Ego, and with our present knowledge of its psychology, much pain and calamity can be averted by proper treatment and re-integration. The fatal impulse to suicide which is characteristic of some temperaments and against which they may have to fight a whole lifetime, is due primarily to a weakened sense of Self. Whether deliberate or involuntary, it represents a struggle between the natural instinct of conservation and a feeling that life is insupportable and not worth while.

It is not, to my mind, a *moral* matter—every human being has the inalienable right to do with his life as he pleases; but it is sad indeed, because so unnecessary and so contrary to the law of progression through experience, to find the sense of Self so deficient as to lead to the very negation of life itself. The self-assertive person feels his power; the more negative character, or one rendered so by the separation and conflict between various phases in his own personality, delivers himself over to a feeling of weakness, denying Self at its very source, and thus defeats the purpose of his existence here.

We have in the previous chapters analyzed the principal forces at work.in the human mind. Let us now suppose a personality made up of these different elements that is so well-proportioned and blended as to be *ideal* in character. Above all it would represent *balance* and *poise* —traits that can be acquired in no other way than by a proper *fusion* and *equilibrium* between Will, Intellect, Emotion and all the other ingredients that go to make up a personality. If the Will, for instance, is too strong in proportion, the nature is hard, over-bearing, and insistent; if the Intellect predominates, it is cold, dry, and critical; and if Emotions are in the ascendancy, it is soft, vague, and impulsive. When, however, all these attributes are united and balanced there is strength, brilliance, and beauty.

Next to *balance* let us place the *sense of Self*

as the most essential foundation of character.
Without self-knowledge the finest qualities are
of little advantage or utility. There must be
an awareness of power and a belief in it; there
must be a well-integrated consciousness equally
active on the three planes of being, *i.e.*, the
spiritual, mental, and physical.

With this as a background we have, first, the
positive element of the *Will* lending force, in-
tegrity, and executiveness to the character—it
forms the "backbone," without which our ideal
would be a spineless phantom: next, the *Emotions* supplying warmth, colour, passion and
propulsion—foremost among which is Sex with
its creativeness, and all the sensibilities that
make for *fineness;* then *Imagination* with its
touch of light and aspiration over all—for the
character that has not its moments of flight and
speculation, that cannot drift at times from the
moorings of the Will into reverie and meditation, is indeed dull and sodden.

But added to all this there must be the tempering and guiding influence of the *Intellect,* the
mechanism by which the sense of Self is raised

into real objectivity and the deep impulses are formed and co-ordinated into a definite focus. With intellectual activity comes the pursuit of Truth for its own sake, research, and the acquisition of knowledge—all of which act as screens upon which are thrown images of that reality which would otherwise remain for ever concealed within. With a true consciousness of Self, the high moral attitude that lifts the character out of inferiority or mediocrity is an inevitable sequence. So too comes a certainty of power, a knowledge of latent depths and how to use them, and a keenness of perception approaching divination. In short the *ideal* character is the *all-inclusive* one which has welcomed its experience, digested it thoroughly, and given back to the world and its Source the full extent of that which it was created to convey.

To be sure, so complete a personality is seldom if ever met with. Life is made up of offshoots and bypaths, and most people are one-sided and unfinished. We swing first in one direction and then the other, gathering strength

from both our successes and our failures.
Naturally our enterprises increase as the arc
of our consciousness expands—and vice versa.

Sometimes the Intellect outruns the moral
sense in its development and we have cleverness, brilliance, "success" without a corresponding elevation in the emotional and spiritual phases; or again we have aspiration and
"saintliness" combined with mental and physical weakness. Very often too, a personality
"breaks down" or disintegrates, through the
buffetings of life—though we know that the
Self remains intact throughout all experience.

Undoubtedly the purpose of experience is to
enable the Self to anneal all the elements of life
into a unity. Experience may come in two
ways; either it *precedes* perception, the knowledge and awareness of a thing coming only
after it has been brought to consciousness by
actual facts or a "living through" it—thus
practical experience leads in time to the form-
ulation of theories, the discovery of laws. Or,
perception may precede *experience,* the consciousness being enabled by some kind of in-

tuition to pierce the barriers of ignorance that surround it and knowledge is obtained as in a vision which may later be put to the test of application—thus do the dreamers work. Usually experience forms the *text-book* of life, of which *reflection* is the commentary. We learn to know of things, really, through *touching* them, but their true significance is borne in upon us later by the judgments of the Intellect and perceptive powers of the mind. A personality is, therefore, very much coloured, first, by the extent of its experience; and second, by its emotional reactions, or the amount of thought and contemplation bestowed upon that experience.

The question of how personalities come to be what they are is, it seems to me, very largely one of the Self. We know, of course, the power of inheritance, but that which is inherited is after all only a *tendency,* due to the fact that *Habits* in one generation become *Instincts* in the next. There are too many variations in the law of heredity to make it a satisfactory and inclusive explanation of the wide varieties of

types and the many exceptions to be observed
on every hand.

Undoubtedly there is in the Self a quality like that of a magnet which attracts to
it certain and definite experiences and which
as surely excludes others. Lives begun under
the same influences become so divergent
that we are forced to look very deep within
for the determining forces. Thus one life
follows lines of quietude and serenity with
little to break or mar it either within or without; while another contains some mysterious but
fiery spark that attracts a wide range of experience, great contrasts, constant movement.
Always the Self is behind these deviations,
drawing with unerring knowledge that which
best conserves its own purposes and welfare.

Also in considering the Self as an entity,
we must not forget that each one has some end
to which he alone is adapted—his quality and
his idiosyncrasies distinguish him from every
other particle in the universe and render him
an essential part of the whole. To those whose
tendency is toward self-depreciation, this

thought is especially valuable. However tied one's hands may seem to be, however many limitations one battles against, we should never forget the *necessity* and the *indestructibility* of the Self.

I will now consider rather briefly a few principal types of personality. There is the ancient classification which was originally physiological but has been more or less used in a psychological sense as well. This consists of the *Sanguine* temperament, reputed to be light, versatile, optimistic, and superficial; the *Melancholic,* which is deep, self-involved, hesitating; the *Choleric,* the intense, active nature with great imagination and tenacious passions, and the *Lymphatic* which is soft and slow, with not much initiative, but great dependability.

These of course, are very general types admitting of endless admixtures. There is for instance the distinctly *unstable* personality which has no special form of its own, takes on the characteristics of its environment, is largely the product of its circumstances, and plastic to excess.

There is another large class quite distinct
from this, with much more intelligence and
strength but which yet suffers from a form of
instability—they are the *sensitives*—emotional
and impressionable in the extreme, like delicate
instruments in a perpetual state of vibration.
In spite of well-developed Intellects their life
is mainly subjective. They form a large proportion of the well known "nervous" temperaments, are often inclined to pessimism, and are
especially liable to the maladies incident to a
disturbed personality.

Then there are those who are instinctively
and unceasingly active, exuberant, over-flowing
with energy. Feeling their strength they are
usually optimistic, gay, enterprising, bold; but
unless characterized also by unusual intelligence, lack in the necessary steadiness and reserve.

In many ways, however, the active ones are
like the emotional type, which is quick, volatile,
acts upon impulse and is guided largely by intuition. It is attractive, possesses warm and
intense feelings, but does not always sustain

them. Its activity has its own special characteristic of being intermittent or spasmodic, arising as it does from strong emotions and not from permanent reserves of energy. It is indolent and energetic by turns and requires periods of solitude in which to recover after its characteristic and impetuous outbursts. To this group belong most of the artists and creative workers, who accomplish things by "inspiration" or unconscious impulse; then undergoing periods of exhaustion and impotence. Because more marked in its characteristics this type is frequently said to have "temperament" —the word really conveying our idea of the *crescendo* that is characteristic of any vivid personality.

In contrast to all this is the lymphatic temperament, distinguished by a certain apathy tending to inertia; they are indifferent rather than plastic. When the intelligence is low they are sluggish and incapable; with a high degree of Intellect they evince the greatest reliability and because of the absence of excitability are able to plan and calculate to great advantage.

They may have very deep feelings, but do not
show them; and they cannot be moved or persuaded by external influences. They are more
often contemplative than active, and constitute
what may be called the *moral* temperaments—
may even become stoics.

Much unhappiness could be avoided if we
would only permit people the luxury of their
own peculiarities and not desire so ardently to
make them over according to our own mould.
This world would be a poor place without the
stimulus of diversity, yet each one of us instinctively desires to make it all over on his
own pattern. If this constructive impulse were
devoted to *making ourselves over,* seeking a
rounded development inclusive of all types and
temperaments, things would be better.

Each man's gait, look and behaviour reveals all his private history—these things
are a kaleidoscopic commentary on his
age, station and quality; they change as he
changes, and can be neither hurried nor delayed.
If he accepts a new fact or truth and acts upon
it, it is because he is ready for it, and cannot

be denied; if he passes by with eyes closed he has only published his immaturity.

The antiquity of the soul, or how many forms it has ascended through, cannot be concealed. Elevation of character, graciousness of manner, poise and balance, strength and power, are all unerring indicators of how far one has progressed in life's unending cycle.

That this passage of the soul through eternity may be accelerated by man's own awakening consciousness of Self, all nature conspires to tell us. Self-culture, in its true sense, that is, for high ends, is man's most noble occupation.

"A great Idealist never can be egotistic," says Ruskin. "The whole of his power depends upon his losing sight and feeling of his own existence, and becoming a mere witness and mirror of truth, and a scribe of visions—always passive in sight, passive in utterance, lamenting continually that he cannot completely reflect nor clearly utter all he has seen—not by any means a proud state for a man to be in. It is the man who has no invention who is always setting things in order, and putting the world to rights, and mending, and beautifying, and pluming himself on his doings, as supreme in all ways.''

Hence, the culture of the Self lifts one above all pettiness, minimizes the importance of the personal ''me,'' and supplies an impregnable support. It provides a perception of the inexhaustibleness of nature—which is the secret of immortal youth. It obliterates the sense of struggle, wipes out convulsions, despair, and the gnashing of teeth—in short, it is the only path to liberation and high behaviour.

Printed in the United States
99262LV00006B/143/A

9 781428 637399